From the Heart - Father of the Bride Speeches

Jonathan Marks

Published by Jonathan Marks, 2024.

While every precaution has been taken in the preparation of this book, the publisher assumes no responsibility for errors or omissions, or for damages resulting from the use of the information contained herein.

FROM THE HEART - FATHER OF THE BRIDE SPEECHES

First edition. February 27, 2024.

Written by Jonathan Marks.

From the Heart: Father-of-the-Bride Speeches

Welcome to "From the Heart: Father of the Bride Speeches." This book is a comprehensive, heartfelt guide designed to help fathers craft memorable and meaningful speeches for their daughter's wedding day.

As a father, delivering a speech at your daughter's wedding is momentous. It's a time to reflect on the journey you've shared with your daughter, to celebrate her love and happiness, and to offer words of wisdom and guidance as she embarks on this new chapter of her life.

In "From the Heart," you'll find a wealth of inspiration, guidance, and practical tips to help you create a speech reflecting your love and affection for your daughter. From crafting the perfect opening lines to delivering a heartfelt toast, this book covers every aspect of writing and delivering a memorable father-of-the-bride speech.

Whether you're a seasoned public speaker or someone nervous at the thought of addressing a crowd, "From the Heart" is here to help. With step-by-step instructions, real-life examples, and expert advice, you'll learn how to express your emotions with sincerity and authenticity, leaving a lasting impression on your daughter, her partner, and everyone else in attendance.

So, grab a pen, take a deep breath, and start creating a speech straight from the heart. After all, there's no greater gift you can give your daughter on her wedding day than words spoken with love, sincerity, and from the depths of your heart.

Chapter 1 – Crafting Heartfelt Memories: The Father of the Bride Speech-Making Process

1. Gather Information: Gather information about the wedding, such as the date, venue, and theme. You should also gather details about the bride and groom, including their personalities, interests, and any special memories or anecdotes you want to include in your speech.
2. Define Your Message: Decide on the main message you want to convey in your speech. Do you want to share heartfelt memories, offer advice and blessings, or express your love and pride for your daughter? Clarifying your message will help guide the content and structure of your speech.
3. Write an Outline: Create a simple outline for your speech, including an introduction, body, and conclusion. In the introduction, welcome guests and establish the purpose of your speech. The body should include your main points, such as sharing memories, offering advice, and expressing love and pride. Finally, the conclusion should wrap up your speech with a heartfelt toast or blessing for the newlyweds.
4. Brainstorm Ideas: Take some time to brainstorm ideas for your speech. Reflect on your relationship with your daughter, memorable moments you've shared together, and any special qualities or characteristics you want to highlight. You can also draw inspiration from family traditions, cultural customs, or favourite quotes and poems.
5. Write the Speech: Begin writing your speech using your outline and brainstorm ideas as a guide. Start with a warm welcome and introduction, then transition into heartfelt memories, offering advice, and expressing love and

pride for your daughter. Write conversationally and use personal anecdotes and examples to connect with your audience.

6. Edit and Revise: Once you've written a draft of your speech, take time to edit and revise it for clarity, coherence, and flow. Remove unnecessary details or tangents, and make sure your message is concise and focused. Pay attention to grammar, punctuation, and spelling errors, and make any necessary corrections.

7. Practice Delivery: Practice delivering your speech aloud several times to become familiar with the content and flow. Pay attention to your tone, pace, and gestures, and adjust as needed. Practice in front of a mirror or with a trusted friend or family member who can provide feedback and encouragement.

8. Seek Feedback: Once you've practiced your speech, seek feedback from others who can offer constructive criticism and suggestions for improvement. Consider asking family members, friends, or members of the wedding party for their input, and be open to making revisions based on their feedback.

9. Finalize Your Speech: Make any final revisions or adjustments to your speech based on feedback and practice sessions. Once you're satisfied with the content and delivery, finalize your speech and prepare to deliver it at the wedding.

10. Deliver Your Speech: On the wedding day, take a deep breath, relax, and focus on delivering your speech with sincerity and confidence. Remember to speak slowly and clearly, make eye contact with the audience, and convey your message from the heart. Enjoy this special moment with your daughter and the newlyweds and savour the memories you'll create together.

Following this step-by-step process, you can craft a heartfelt and memorable speech as the bride's father, celebrating your daughter's special day and leaving a lasting impression on everyone in attendance.

Chapter 2 Mastering the Moment: Overcoming Nerves for the Father of the Bride Speech

As the bride's father, delivering a speech at your daughter's wedding is a momentous occasion filled with emotion, pride, and joy. However, it's also natural to experience nerves and anxiety leading up to the big moment. Speaking in front of a crowd, expressing your emotions, and making your daughter proud can be overwhelming. But fear not, because you can overcome your nerves with the right preparation and mindset and deliver a heartfelt and memorable speech that celebrates your daughter's special day. Here's how:

1. Acknowledge Your Feelings: Feeling nervous before giving a speech is normal, especially on such an important occasion. Instead of trying to ignore or suppress your feelings, acknowledge them and accept them as a natural part of the process. Remember that nerves are simply a sign that you care deeply about the moment and want to do your best.

2. Prepare Thoroughly: One of the most effective ways to overcome nerves is through thorough preparation. Take the time to carefully plan and craft your speech, including outlining your main points, writing out your thoughts, and rehearsing your delivery. Practice in front of a mirror, record yourself, or enlist the help of a friend or family member to provide feedback. The more prepared you are, the more confident you'll feel when it's time to speak.

3. Know Your Material: Familiarize yourself with the content of your speech so that you can speak confidently and naturally. Practice reciting your speech until you feel comfortable with the flow and wording. Consider using note cards or a written

outline as a reference during your speech but aim to deliver your message without relying too heavily on them. Knowing your material inside and out will give you the confidence to speak from the heart.

4. Visualize Success: Take a few moments to visualize yourself delivering your speech with confidence and poise. Picture yourself standing tall, making eye contact with the audience, and speaking with clarity and conviction. Visualizing success can help calm your nerves and build your confidence as you mentally rehearse the speech in your mind.

5. Focus on Your Message: Shift your focus away from your nerves and instead concentrate on the message you want to convey. Remember that your speech is an opportunity to celebrate your daughter's love and happiness, express your pride and joy, and offer words of wisdom and encouragement for her future. By keeping your attention on the meaning behind your words, you'll be able to speak with authenticity and sincerity.

6. Take Deep Breaths: Practice deep breathing techniques to help calm your nerves and centre yourself before speaking. Take slow, deep breaths in through your nose, hold for a few seconds, and then exhale slowly through your mouth. Repeat this process several times to relax your body and clear your mind.

7. Embrace Imperfection: Understand that it's okay to be imperfect and make mistakes during your speech. No one expects you to deliver a flawless performance, and small errors or hiccups are a natural part of public speaking. Instead of striving for perfection, focus on being genuine and authentic in your delivery. Your daughter and the guests will appreciate your sincerity and heartfelt words, regardless of any minor slip-ups.

8. Stay Present: As you step up to deliver your speech, focus on staying present in the moment. Concentrate on the here and now instead of letting your mind wander to worries or distractions. Take a moment to look around the room, make eye contact with your daughter and other loved ones, and soak in the occasion's significance. By staying present, you'll be able to fully experience and enjoy the moment as it unfolds.

9. Practice Relaxation Techniques: Incorporate relaxation techniques into your pre-speech routine to help calm your nerves and centre yourself. Techniques such as progressive muscle relaxation, visualization, or mindfulness meditation can help reduce anxiety and increase your sense of calmness and control.

10. Remember Your Purpose: Above all, remember that your speech is a gift to your daughter—a chance to celebrate her love and happiness, express your pride and joy, and offer wisdom and encouragement for her future. Keep your focus on the love you share with your daughter and the significance of the moment and let that guide you as you deliver your speech.

By following these tips and techniques, you can overcome your nerves and deliver a heartfelt and memorable speech as the bride's father. Trust in your preparation, focus on your message, and remember to enjoy the moment—it's a once-in-a-lifetime opportunity to celebrate your daughter's love and happiness.

Chapter 3 – Speeches from the Heart

"A Father's Love: A Heartfelt Tribute to My Daughter"

My beloved daughter,

As I stand before you today, surrounded by our loved ones and bathed in the warm glow of this beautiful celebration, my heart overflows with love and pride. From the moment you came into this world, you captured my heart with your radiant smile and boundless spirit. Watching you grow into the remarkable woman you are today has been the greatest joy of my life, and I am filled with gratitude for the privilege of being your father.

You brought light and laughter into our home from your earliest days, filling each moment with joy and wonder. I still remember the sound of your laughter echoing through the halls, the sparkle in your eyes as you discovered the world around you, and the warmth of your embrace as you nestled in my arms. You were always a force to be reckoned with, my dear, a bright and shining star in the tapestry of our lives.

As you grew, so too did your spirit of curiosity and adventure. You approached each day with an open heart and a fearless spirit, eager to explore the world and discover all its wonders. Whether climbing trees in the backyard, chasing butterflies in the garden, or dreaming up elaborate tales with your beloved stuffed animals, you approached each moment with boundless enthusiasm and an infectious zest for life.

But it wasn't just your sense of adventure that captivated me, my dear—it was your kindness, compassion, and unwavering empathy for others. You have always had a heart as big as the sky, my darling, and you've never hesitated to extend a helping hand to those in need. Whether it was comforting a friend in times of sorrow, standing up for what is right, or simply lending a listening ear, you have always exemplified the true meaning of compassion and kindness.

And oh, how you've grown, my precious daughter, into a woman of strength, courage, and grace. You've faced your share of challenges and obstacles along the way, but you've always approached them with resilience, determination, and unwavering faith in yourself. You've shown the world what it means to persevere in the face of adversity, to rise above life's challenges, and to emerge stronger and more resilient on the other side.

Today, as I stand before you, surrounded by family and friends, I am filled with pride and gratitude. You have blossomed into an extraordinary woman, my dear, and I couldn't be more proud of the person you've become. You've overcome obstacles, pursued your dreams with passion and determination, and embraced life with an open heart and a fearless spirit. You've touched the lives of so many with your kindness, compassion, and unwavering love, and you've left an indelible mark on the world around you.

As you embark on this new chapter of your life, my precious daughter, know that you carry with you the love, support, and unwavering belief of everyone gathered here today. You are surrounded by family and friends who cherish you, celebrate you, and believe in you with all their hearts. And as you take this next step on your journey, know that I am here for you, always and forever, cheering you on, supporting you, and loving you with all my heart.

May your marriage be filled with love, laughter, and joy, my dear, and may your life together be as beautiful and radiant as you are. You are my greatest treasure, shining star, and joy; I am so incredibly blessed to be your father.

With all my love and pride,
Your Father

***

"Cherished Memories: A Father's Tribute to His Daughter"
My beloved daughter,

As I stand before you today, surrounded by the ones we hold dear, my heart is filled with a flood of memories—memories of a childhood filled with laughter, love, and boundless joy. From the moment you came into this world, you brought light and warmth into our lives, and I have cherished every moment of watching you grow into the remarkable woman you are today.

I remember the day you were born as if it were yesterday—the overwhelming sense of joy and wonder as I held you in my arms for the very first time. You were so tiny and fragile, yet even in those early moments, you possessed a strength and resilience that took my breath away. From that moment on, I knew that you were destined for greatness, my dear, and I have watched with pride as you've grown into the extraordinary woman you are today.

As a child, you were a whirlwind of energy and curiosity, always eager to explore the world around you and discover its many wonders. I remember our countless hours together, playing in the backyard, building sandcastles at the beach, and embarking on grand adventures in our imaginations. Whether we were chasing fireflies on warm summer nights or cozying up with a book by the fire on cold winter evenings, each moment we shared was filled with love, laughter, and boundless joy.

One of my fondest memories of your childhood is the way you would light up with excitement whenever we embarked on one of our many family adventures. Whether it was a trip to the zoo, a hike in the mountains, or a day at the amusement park, you approached each new experience with wide-eyed wonder and unbridled enthusiasm. Your zest for life was infectious, my dear, and it brought a sense of joy and adventure to even the simplest of outings.

But it wasn't just the big moments that I cherish, my precious daughter—it was the small, everyday moments that truly made our bond special. I remember the way you would wrap your tiny hand around my finger as we walked together, the sound of your laughter echoing through the halls as we played games together, and the warmth of your hugs as you nestled in my arms at bedtime. Those simple, ordinary moments are the ones that I hold closest to my heart, for they are the moments that truly defined our relationship and shaped the person you've become.

As you grew older, your interests and passions began to take shape, and I marvelled at the incredible person you were becoming. Whether you were pursuing your love of music, art, or sports, you approached each new endeavour with determination, dedication, and an unwavering commitment to excellence. Your resilience in the face of adversity, your courage to chase your dreams, and your unwavering belief in yourself have always inspired me, my dear, and I am endlessly proud of the person you've become.

Today, as I stand before you, surrounded by family and friends, I am filled with an overwhelming sense of gratitude for the countless memories we've shared and the bond we've formed over the years. Though the years may pass, and our lives may change, know that the love and memories we've shared will always remain etched in my heart, a testament to the incredible journey we've embarked on together.

As you embark on this new chapter of your life, my precious daughter, know that you carry with you the love, support, and unwavering belief of everyone gathered here today. You are surrounded by family and friends who cherish you, celebrate you, and believe in you with all their hearts. And as you take this next step on your journey, know that I am here for you, always and forever, cheering you on, supporting you, and loving you with all my heart.

May your marriage be filled with love, laughter, and joy, my dear, and may your life together be as beautiful and radiant as you are. You are my greatest treasure, my shining star, and my greatest joy, and I am so incredibly blessed to be your father.

With all my love and fondest memories,
Your Father

*****

"A Lifetime of Memories: A Father's Reflections on His Daughter's Journey"

My beloved daughter,

As I stand before you today, surrounded by the ones we hold dear, my heart is filled with a lifetime of memories—memories of the countless moments we've shared, the laughter we've shared, the tears we've shed, and the bond that has grown between us over the years. Today, as we celebrate this joyous occasion, I reflect on those special moments we've shared and their profound impact on my life.

From the very beginning, you captured my heart with your infectious laughter, your boundless energy, and your unwavering spirit. I still remember the day you took your first steps, your laughter as you chased butterflies in the garden, and the warmth of your embrace as you nestled in my arms at bedtime. Each moment we shared was filled with love, laughter, and a sense of wonder, and I treasured every precious moment we spent together.

As you grew older, our bond only grew stronger, as we navigated life's ups and downs together, supporting each other through the challenges and celebrating the triumphs. Whether we were embarking on family adventures, sharing quiet moments at home, or simply enjoying each other's company, our love and connection were always present, binding us together in a bond that could never be broken.

One of the most special moments we shared was the day you graduated from high school. As I watched you walk across that stage, with your head held high and your heart full of dreams, I felt an overwhelming sense of pride and joy. It was a moment that marked the culmination of years of hard work, dedication, and perseverance, and I couldn't have been more proud of the incredible young woman you had become.

Another cherished memory is the day you embarked on your first solo adventure, venturing out into the world to pursue your dreams. Though it was difficult to watch you spread your wings and fly, I knew that you were ready to take on the world, armed with courage, resilience, and an unwavering belief in yourself. It was a moment that filled me with both pride and sadness, as I realized that my little girl was all grown up and ready to forge her own path in life.

But perhaps the most special moments we've shared together are the quiet, ordinary moments that make up the fabric of our everyday lives. Whether we were sharing a meal together, taking a walk in the park, or simply spending time together at home, those moments were always filled with love, laughter, and a deep sense of connection. They are the moments that I hold closest to my heart, for they are the moments that truly defined our relationship and shaped the person you've become.

Today, as I stand before you, surrounded by family and friends, I am filled with an overwhelming sense of gratitude for the countless memories we've shared and the bond we've formed over the years. Though the years may pass, and our lives may change, the love and memories we've shared will always remain etched in my heart, a testament to the incredible journey we've embarked on together.

As you embark on this new chapter of your life, my precious daughter, know that you carry the love, support, and unwavering belief of everyone gathered here today. You are surrounded by family and friends who cherish you, celebrate you, and believe in you with all their hearts. And as you take this next step on your journey, know that I am here for you, always and forever, cheering you on, supporting you, and loving you with all my heart.

May your marriage be filled with love, laughter, and joy, my dear, and may your life together be as beautiful and radiant as you are. You are my greatest treasure, my shining star, and my greatest joy, and I am so incredibly blessed to be your father.

With all my love and fondest memories,
Your Father

***

"A Father's Wisdom: Navigating Life's Journey with Love and Guidance"

My dearest daughter,

As I stand before you today, surrounded by our loved ones and bathed in the warm glow of this beautiful celebration, my heart swells with love and pride. From the moment you came into this world, you have been a beacon of light and joy in my life, and I am endlessly grateful for the privilege of being your father. Today, as you embark on this new chapter of your life, I want to share with you some words of wisdom and advice that I hope will guide you as you navigate the journey ahead.

First and foremost, my dear, remember the importance of staying true to yourself. In a world that can sometimes feel overwhelming and uncertain, it's easy to lose sight of who you are and what you believe in. But never forget that you are a unique and extraordinary individual, with your gifts and talents alone. Embrace your uniqueness, celebrate your strengths, and never be afraid to stand up for what you believe in, even in the face of adversity.

As you journey through life, my precious daughter, remember to always follow your heart and pursue your passions with courage and determination. Whether you dream of traveling the world, pursuing a career that fills you with purpose, or starting a family of your own, never let fear or doubt hold you back from chasing your dreams. Trust in yourself, believe in your abilities, and know that you have the power to create the life you've always imagined.

But while it's important to pursue your dreams and ambitions, my dear, remember to also take time to nurture your relationships and cultivate meaningful connections with those you love. Your family and friends are your greatest treasures in life, and the love and support they offer will sustain you through life's joys and challenges. Cherish the moments you share with your loved ones, make time for the people who matter most to you, and never take their love for granted.

In the years ahead, my precious daughter, you will undoubtedly face your share of challenges and obstacles but remember that every setback is an opportunity for growth and learning. Embrace life's challenges with resilience and determination and use them as opportunities to discover your own strength and resilience. Remember that you can overcome any obstacle that comes your way, and that every setback is simply a stepping stone on the path to success.

And finally, my dear, never forget the importance of kindness, compassion, and empathy in everything you do. In a world that can sometimes feel cold and indifferent, the simple act of showing kindness and compassion to others can make a world of difference. Treat others with respect and empathy, lend a helping hand to those in need, and strive to make the world a better place through your words and actions.

As you embark on this new chapter of your life, my precious daughter, know that you carry with you the love, support, and unwavering belief of everyone gathered here today. You are surrounded by family and friends who cherish you, celebrate you, and believe in you with all their hearts. And as you take this next step on your journey, know that I am here for you, always and forever, cheering you on, supporting you, and loving you with all my heart.

May your marriage be filled with love, laughter, and joy, my dear, and may your life together be as beautiful and radiant as you are. You are my greatest treasure, shining star, and joy; I am so incredibly blessed to be your father.

With all my love and words of wisdom,

Your Father

***

"Gratitude and Joy: A Father's Heartfelt Tribute to His Daughter"

My dearest daughter,

As I stand before you today, surrounded by our cherished family and friends, my heart is filled with gratitude and joy. From the moment you came into this world, you have been a source of immeasurable happiness and love in my life, and I am endlessly grateful for the gift of being your father. Today, as we gather to celebrate this joyous occasion, I want to take a moment to express my deepest gratitude for the joy and happiness you have brought into my life.

From the very beginning, you captured my heart with your infectious laughter, your boundless energy, and your radiant smile. I still remember the first time I held you in my arms, feeling the weight of your tiny body and marvelling at the miracle of life I held. At that moment, I knew that you were destined for greatness, and I vowed to cherish and protect you with all my heart.

As you grew older, our bond only grew stronger, as we shared countless moments of laughter, love, and joy together. Whether we were embarking on family adventures, sharing quiet moments at home, or simply enjoying each other's company, our love and connection were always present, binding us together in a bond that could never be broken.

One of the greatest joys of my life has been watching you grow into the remarkable woman you are today. You possess a strength, grace, and beauty that takes my breath away, and I couldn't be more proud of the person you've become. Your kindness, compassion, and unwavering spirit are a testament to the incredible person you are, and I am endlessly grateful for the joy and happiness you bring into my life every day.

Today, as we celebrate this joyous occasion, I want to take a moment to express my deepest gratitude for the countless memories we've shared and the bond we've formed over the years. Though the years may pass, and our lives may change, know that the love and joy you bring into my life will always remain etched in my heart, a testament to the incredible journey we've embarked on together.

As you embark on this new chapter of your life, my precious daughter, know that you carry with you the love, support, and unwavering belief of everyone gathered here today. You are surrounded by family and friends who cherish you, celebrate you, and believe in you with all their hearts. And as you take this next step on your journey, know that I am here for you, always and forever, cheering you on, supporting you, and loving you with all my heart.

May your marriage be filled with love, laughter, and joy, my dear, and may your life together be as beautiful and radiant as you are. You are my greatest treasure, my shining star, and my greatest joy, and I am endlessly grateful for the gift of being your father.

With all my love and deepest gratitude,

Your Father

***

"Grateful for the Journey: A Father's Tribute to His Daughter"

My dearest daughter,

As I stand before you today, surrounded by our cherished family and friends, my heart is filled with an overwhelming sense of gratitude and pride. From the moment you came into this world, you have been a beacon of light and joy in my life, and I am endlessly grateful for the gift of being your father. Today, as we gather to celebrate this joyous occasion, I want to take a moment to express my deepest gratitude for the incredible person you have become.

From your earliest days, you captured my heart with your infectious laughter, your boundless curiosity, and your unwavering spirit. I still remember the first time I held you in my arms, feeling the weight of your tiny body and marvelling at the miracle of life that I held in my hands. At that moment, I knew that you were destined for greatness, and I vowed to cherish and protect you with all my heart.

As you grew older, your spirit of curiosity and adventure grew stronger, as you fearlessly pursued your dreams and embraced life's many adventures with open arms. Whether exploring the world around you, pursuing your passions with determination and dedication, or standing up for what you believe in, you approach each new experience with courage, resilience, and an unwavering belief in yourself.

One of the greatest joys of my life has been watching you grow into the remarkable woman you are today. You possess a strength, grace, and beauty that takes my breath away, and I couldn't be more proud of the person you have become. Your kindness, compassion, and unwavering spirit are a testament to the incredible person you are, and I am endlessly grateful for the joy and inspiration you bring into my life every day.

Today, as we celebrate this joyous occasion, I want to take a moment to express my deepest gratitude for the journey we have shared together. Though the years may pass, and our lives may change, know that the love and connection we share will always remain etched in my heart, a testament to the incredible bond we have formed over the years.

As you embark on this new chapter of your life, my precious daughter, know that you carry with you the love, support, and unwavering belief of everyone gathered here today. You are surrounded by family and friends who cherish you, celebrate you, and believe in you with all their hearts. And as you take this next step on your journey, know that I am here for you, always and forever, cheering you on, supporting you, and loving you with all my heart.

May your marriage be filled with love, laughter, and joy, my dear, and may your life together be as beautiful and radiant as you are. You are my greatest treasure, my shining star, and my greatest joy, and I am endlessly grateful for the gift of being your father.

With all my love and deepest gratitude,
Your Father

***

"Celebrating Milestones: A Father's Reflection on His Daughter's Achievements"

My beloved daughter,

As I stand before you today, surrounded by our cherished family and friends, my heart swells with pride and joy. From the moment you came into this world, you have filled our lives with love, laughter, and countless precious memories. Today, as we celebrate this joyous occasion, I want to take a moment to reminisce about the milestones and accomplishments that have shaped the remarkable woman you are today.

From your very first steps to your graduation day, each milestone you reached was a cause for celebration and a testament to your determination, perseverance, and unwavering spirit. I still remember your look of sheer delight as you took those tentative first steps, your eyes sparkling with excitement and anticipation. It was a moment of pure joy and wonder, and it marked the beginning of a journey filled with countless adventures and achievements.

As you grew older, you continued to reach new heights and accomplish great things, each milestone a testament to your resilience, courage, and unwavering commitment to excellence. Whether it was excelling in school, pursuing your passions with passion and dedication, or overcoming obstacles with grace and determination, you approached each new challenge with courage and determination, never letting fear or doubt hold you back from reaching your goals.

One of the proudest moments of my life was watching you graduate from high school, your head held high and your heart full of dreams. It was a moment that marked the culmination of years of hard work, dedication, and perseverance, and I couldn't have been more proud of the incredible young woman you had become. As you stood on that stage, surrounded by your classmates and loved ones, I knew that you were destined for greatness, and I vowed to support you in every way possible as you embarked on the next chapter of your journey.

And oh, how you've grown and flourished since that day, my dear daughter. From pursuing your dreams with passion and determination to overcoming obstacles with grace and resilience, you have proven time and time again that you are capable of achieving anything you set your mind to. Whether it's pursuing your career goals, traveling the world, or starting a family of your own, I have no doubt that you will continue to accomplish great things and positively impact the world around you.

Today, as we celebrate this joyous occasion, I want to take a moment to express my deepest gratitude for the milestones and accomplishments that have shaped the remarkable person you are today. Though the years may pass, and our lives may change, the pride and joy I feel in being your father will always remain unwavering, a testament to the incredible journey we have embarked on together.

As you embark on this new chapter of your life, my precious daughter, know that you carry with you the love, support, and unwavering belief of everyone gathered here today. You are surrounded by family and friends who cherish you, celebrate you, and believe in you with all their hearts. And as you take this next step on your journey, know that I am here for you, always and forever, cheering you on, supporting you, and loving you with all my heart.

May your marriage be filled with love, laughter, and joy, my dear, and may your life together be as beautiful and radiant as you are. You are my greatest treasure, my shining star, and my greatest joy, and I am endlessly proud of the person you have become.

With all my love and deepest pride,
Your Father

***

"Unwavering Support: A Father's Promise to His Daughter"

My dearest daughter,

As I stand before you today, surrounded by our cherished family and friends, my heart is filled with an overwhelming sense of love, pride, and gratitude. From the moment you came into this world, you have been a source of immeasurable joy and happiness in my life, and I am endlessly grateful for the privilege of being your father. Today, as we celebrate this joyous occasion and mark the beginning of this new chapter in your life, I want to offer you my unwavering support and encouragement as you embark on this incredible journey.

As you stand on the threshold of this new chapter, my precious daughter, know that you carry the love, support, and unwavering belief of everyone gathered here today. You are surrounded by family and friends who cherish you, celebrate you, and believe in you with all their hearts. And as you take this next step on your journey, know that I am here for you, always and forever, cheering you on, supporting you, and loving you with all my heart.

As you embark on this new chapter of your life, my precious daughter, know that you carry the love, support, and unwavering belief of everyone gathered here today. You are surrounded by family and friends who cherish you, celebrate you, and believe in you with all their hearts. And as you take this next step on your journey, know that I am here for you, always and forever, cheering you on, supporting you, and loving you with all my heart.

May your marriage be filled with love, laughter, and joy, my dear, and may your life together be as beautiful and radiant as you are. You are my greatest treasure, shining star, and joy, and I am endlessly proud of the person you have become.

With all my love and deepest pride,

Your Father

***

"Dreams for Tomorrow: A Father's Heartfelt Wishes for His Daughter"
   My dearest daughter,
   As I stand before you today, surrounded by the ones we hold dear, my heart is filled with an abundance of love, pride, and hope for the future. Since you came into this world, you have been a beacon of light and joy in my life, filling each day with laughter, love, and countless precious memories. Today, as we celebrate this joyous occasion and mark the beginning of this new chapter in your life, I want to share with you my deepest hopes and dreams for the journey that lies ahead.

   As you embark on this new chapter of your life, my precious daughter, know that you carry with you the hopes and dreams of everyone gathered here today. You are surrounded by family and friends who cherish you, celebrate you, and believe in you with all their hearts. And as you take this next step on your journey, know that I am here for you, always and forever, cheering you on, supporting you, and loving you with all my heart.

   First and foremost, my dear daughter, I hope that you find true happiness and fulfilment in all that you do. May your days be filled with laughter and joy, and your heart be filled with love and gratitude for the blessings surrounding you. Whether you're pursuing your passions, building a career, or starting a family of your own, my greatest wish for you is that you find happiness and contentment in every aspect of your life.

   I also hope that you find strength and resilience in the face of life's challenges and setbacks. Though the road ahead may be filled with twists and turns, know that you can overcome any obstacle that comes your way. Draw strength from the love and support of those who cherish you, and never lose sight of the incredible resilience and determination that lies within you.

   My precious daughter, I hope that you never lose sight of the incredible person you are and the limitless potential that lies within you. You can achieve anything you set your mind to, my dear, and I have no doubt that you will accomplish great things in the years to come. Whether you're pursuing your dreams, making a difference in the lives of others, or simply living life to the fullest, remember that you can achieve anything you set your mind to.

As you embark on this new chapter of your life, my precious daughter, know that you carry with you the love, support, and unwavering belief of everyone gathered here today. You are surrounded by family and friends who cherish you, celebrate you, and believe in you with all their hearts. And as you take this next step on your journey, know that I am here for you, always and forever, cheering you on, supporting you, and loving you with all my heart.

May your marriage be filled with love, laughter, and joy, my dear, and may your life together be as beautiful and radiant as you are. You are my greatest treasure, shining star, and joy, and I am endlessly proud of the person you have become.

With all my love,

Your Father

***

"A Father's Embrace: Words of Reassurance and Comfort on Your Wedding Day"

My dearest daughter,

As I stand before you today, my heart swells with love, pride, and nostalgia. It seems like just yesterday that I held you in my arms for the first time, marvelling at the miracle of life that I held in my hands. And now, as I watch you stand before me, radiant and resplendent in your wedding gown, I am filled with an overwhelming sense of love and gratitude for the incredible woman you have become.

Today, as we celebrate this joyous occasion and mark the beginning of this new chapter in your life, I want to offer you my words of reassurance and comfort as you embark on this incredible journey. My precious daughter, know that you are surrounded by love, support, and unwavering belief from everyone gathered here today, and as you take this next step on your journey, know that I am here for you, always and forever, cheering you on, supporting you, and loving you with all my heart.

As you stand on the threshold of this new chapter in your life, my dear daughter, know that you are embarking on a journey filled with love, laughter, and countless precious memories. Though the road ahead may be filled with twists and turns, know that you can overcome any obstacle that comes your way. Draw strength from the love and support of those who cherish you, and never lose sight of the incredible resilience and determination within you.

As you embark on this new chapter of your life, my precious daughter, know that you carry with you the love, support, and unwavering belief of everyone gathered here today. You are surrounded by family and friends who cherish you, celebrate you, and believe in you with all their hearts. And as you take this next step on your journey, know that I am here for you, always and forever, cheering you on, supporting you, and loving you with all my heart.

May your marriage be filled with love, laughter, and joy, my dear, and may your life together be as beautiful and radiant as you are. You are my greatest treasure, shining star, and joy, and I am endlessly proud of the person you have become.

With all my love and deepest pride,

Your Father

***

"A Father's Reflection: Witnessing Her Joyful Journey to Love"

As I stand here, watching her radiant smile as she dances with her beloved, my heart swells with indescribable joy. It's a moment I've envisioned countless times, yet the reality surpasses any imagination. As the bride's father, I am overwhelmed by the profound happiness that fills the air, knowing that she has found love, and more importantly, profound happiness.

Reflecting on the journey that brought us to this moment, I am reminded of the years that have passed years filled with laughter, tears, and countless cherished memories. From her first steps to her graduation day, I've been privileged to witness every milestone, every triumph, and every challenge. Yet, amidst it all, there was always a silent wish in my heart: to see her find someone who would cherish her as much as I do and bring out the best in her and stand by her through life's ups and downs.

And now, as I gaze upon her glowing face, hand in hand with the one who has captured her heart, I am filled with an overwhelming sense of gratitude. Gratitude for the journey that has led us here, and gratitude for the person who has chosen to embark on this journey with her. For in his eyes, I see a love that is pure and unwavering—a love that mirrors the depth of my own for her.

As a father, there is perhaps no greater joy than witnessing your child find love and happiness. It's a joy that transcends words, a feeling that resonates deep within your soul. And in this moment, surrounded by family and friends who have come together to celebrate this union, I am reminded of the power of love to bring people together, to heal wounds, and to inspire hope.

But amidst the celebration, there is also a bittersweet realization—that with this union comes a new chapter in which she will build a life of her own, separate from the one she has known. And while part of me longs to hold onto her childhood memories, I know that it is time to let go, to trust in the love that has brought her to this moment, and to embrace the future with open arms.

Love is not about holding on tightly; it's about letting go and allowing the ones we love to spread their wings and soar. As I watch her twirl around the dance floor, her laughter echoing in the air, I am filled with a sense of peace that comes from knowing that she has found her soulmate, her life partner.

In the eyes of a father, there is perhaps no greater joy than seeing his daughter find love and happiness. It's a joy that surpasses all others, bringing tears to the eyes and warmth to the heart. And as I look around at the faces of our loved ones, I am reminded of the power of love to unite us, to bring us together in moments of joy and celebration.

As the music fades and the evening draws to a close, I take her hand in mine, whispering a silent prayer for her happiness and well-being. For as long as I live, I will carry with me the memory of this day—the day when I witnessed her find love and happiness, when my heart overflowed with joy and gratitude.

And as we bid farewell to our guests and make our way home, I am filled with a sense of contentment that comes from knowing she is loved, cherished, and truly happy. In the end, isn't that all any parent could ever wish for their child?

***

"Embracing New Beginnings: A Father's Joy in Welcoming His Daughter's Partner"

Ladies and gentlemen, esteemed family and friends,

Today marks a momentous occasion filled with love, joy, and the promise of new beginnings. As the bride's father, I am deeply honoured and profoundly moved to stand before you all, not only to celebrate the union of two souls but also to express my heartfelt excitement in welcoming a new member into our family.

From the moment she entered this world, my daughter has been a beacon of light, filling our lives with laughter, love, and endless moments of wonder. Watching her grow into the remarkable woman she is today has been one of life's greatest blessings—a journey marked by countless cherished memories, shared dreams, and unwavering love.

And now, as I look upon her radiant smile and the hand of the person who has captured her heart, I am filled with an overwhelming sense of joy and gratitude. For in his eyes, I see not only love but also a deep understanding of the extraordinary woman my daughter is—a woman of strength, compassion, and boundless kindness.

To welcome someone new into our family is to embrace the promise of the future, to open our hearts to new experiences, and to create lasting bonds that transcend bloodlines. And as I stand here today, I do so with an immense sense of excitement and anticipation, eager to welcome him into our family with open arms and hearts.

Love knows no boundaries, limitations, or conditions—it is a force that unites us all, binding us together in a tapestry of shared experiences and cherished moments. And in welcoming him into our family, we are not only embracing the love that he brings into my daughter's life but also the love that he extends to every one of us gathered here today.

To my dear daughter's partner, I say this: welcome. Welcome to our family, hearts, and a lifetime filled with love, laughter, and cherished memories. You have captured not only my daughter's heart but also all who know and love her; for that, we are eternally grateful.

As you embark on this journey together, know that you do not walk alone—you walk hand in hand with each other, supported by the love and blessings of those around you. May your days be filled with joy, your hearts with love, and your lives with countless moments of happiness and fulfilment.

And to my dear daughter, I offer these words of love and encouragement: you have always been a source of light and inspiration in our lives, and seeing you find love and happiness fills my heart with immeasurable joy. As you embark on this new chapter of your life, know that you are loved beyond measure, supported unconditionally, and cherished beyond words.

Today, we celebrate the love that binds you together and the love that surrounds you—a love that knows no bounds and no end. May your journey together be filled with laughter, your hearts be forever entwined, and your love grow stronger with each passing day.

In closing, let us raise our glasses to toast the happy couple—to love, to laughter, and a lifetime of shared dreams and cherished moments. May your love shine brightly for all the world to see, and may your hearts be forever filled with the joy of each other's company.

Cheers to love, cheers to happiness, and cheers to the beautiful journey that lies ahead.

Thank you.

***

"Embracing the Sacred Union: A Father's Reflection on Marriage and Commitment"

Ladies and gentlemen, beloved family and friends,

As we gather here today to celebrate the union of two souls, I am deeply honoured to share some reflections on the significance of marriage and commitment. As the bride's father, I stand before you with a heart full of love and gratitude, witnessing this beautiful moment that marks the beginning of a lifelong journey for my daughter and her partner.

Marriage is a sacred bond—a union of hearts, minds, and souls transcending time and space. It is a commitment to stand by each other's side through thick and thin, to share in life's joys and sorrows, and to support each other's dreams and aspirations. But more than that, marriage is a testament to the power of love—the kind of love that knows no bounds, limits, and no end.

In a world filled with constant change and uncertainty, marriage offers a sense of stability, a rock-solid foundation upon which to build a life together. It is a promise to love, honour, and cherish each other, not only in times of happiness but also in times of hardship. It is a vow—a vow to be there for each other, to hold each other up when the world seems to crumble around you and to never waver in your commitment to one another.

But perhaps most importantly, marriage is a journey—a journey of growth, discovery, and transformation. It is a journey that challenges you to become the best version of yourselves, learn from each other, and evolve together as individuals and partners. It is a journey filled with unexpected twists and turns and countless moments of joy, laughter, and love.

As I look upon my daughter and her partner, I am filled with pride and joy. In their love, I see the promise of a future filled with endless possibilities—a future built on mutual respect, understanding, and unwavering devotion. And as they embark on this journey together, I am confident that they will navigate life's challenges with grace and resilience, guided by the love that binds them together.

To my dear daughter and her partner, I offer these words of wisdom and encouragement: cherish each other, honour each other, and never lose sight of the love that brought you together. May your marriage be a source of strength and inspiration, a beacon of hope in times of darkness, and a testament to the power of love to conquer all obstacles?

And to all of you gathered here today, I urge you to reflect on the significance of marriage and commitment in your lives. Whether you are married, engaged, or single, may you always hold fast to the belief in the transformative power of love and never lose sight of the beauty of true partnership.

As we celebrate this joyous occasion, let us raise our glasses to toast the happy couple—to love, commitment, and the sacred bond that unites them as husband and wife. May their love grow stronger with each passing day, and may their marriage be a shining example of the beauty and power of true love.

Thank you.

***

"Blessings for a Lifetime: A Father's Heartfelt Wishes for His Daughter's Marriage"

Ladies and gentlemen, cherished family and friends,

Today, as we gather to witness the union of two souls, I am filled with profound gratitude and joy. As the bride's father, I am honoured to stand before you and offer my heartfelt blessings for my daughter's marriage. This moment, this beautiful occasion, marks the beginning of a new chapter—a chapter filled with love, laughter, and the promise of a lifetime of happiness together.

I speak these words from the depths of my heart to my dearest daughter and her beloved partner. May your marriage be a journey of endless discovery filled with laughter, shared dreams, and the beauty of growing old together. May you always cherish each other's presence, finding solace and comfort in the embrace of your love.

As you embark on this sacred union, may you be guided by respect, trust, and unwavering commitment. May you nurture your relationship with kindness and compassion, understanding that true love is a gift to be cherished and protected. And may you never lose sight of the profound significance of the vows you have made to one another—to love, honour, and cherish each other, for better or for worse, for richer or for poorer, in sickness and in health, until death do you part.

To my daughter, I offer these words of wisdom and encouragement: You are a radiant light in our lives, a beacon of hope and inspiration to all who know you. As you journey through life with your beloved, may you always remember the strength and resilience that lies within you. May you face each challenge with grace and courage, knowing that you are never alone, for you carry the love and support of your family and friends within you.

And to my dear son-in-law, I extend my warmest welcome to our family. You have captured my daughter's heart; for that, I am eternally grateful. As you embark on this journey together, know that you are surrounded by love and blessings from all gathered here today. May you always be a source of strength and support to each other, sharing in life's joys and sorrows with unwavering devotion.

As you build your life together, may you create a home filled with laughter, warmth, and unconditional love. May you nurture your bond with patience and understanding, always striving to see the best in each other and to lift each other up in times of need. May you never lose sight of the magic that brought you together—the spark of love that ignited your souls and set your hearts ablaze with passion and desire.

To the happy couple, I offer these heartfelt blessings: May your marriage be blessed with abundant joy and laughter, peace and harmony, and an unbreakable bond that withstands the test of time. May you continue to grow and evolve together, celebrating each triumph and weathering each storm with grace and resilience. May your love shine brightly for all the world to see, a testament to the power of love to conquer all obstacles and unite hearts in a truly eternal bond.

As we raise our glasses in celebration, let us toast to the love that brings us together today—to the love that knows no bounds and to the love that will guide you on this incredible journey ahead. May your marriage bless all who know you, and may your hearts be forever filled with the joy of each other's company.

Thank you.

***

"A Father's Gratitude: Walking My Daughter Down the Aisle"

Ladies and gentlemen, cherished family and friends,

As I stand before you today, my heart is filled with gratitude and profound emotion. Today is a day I have dreamed of since the moment my daughter came into this world—a day when I have the extraordinary privilege of walking her down the aisle and witnessing her embark on a new chapter of her life.

From the very beginning, my daughter has been my pride and joy—a source of endless love, laughter, and boundless happiness. Watching her grow into the remarkable woman she is today has been the greatest blessing of my life, and I am eternally grateful for every moment we have shared together.

As I reflect on the journey that has brought us to this moment, I am filled with a deep gratitude for the opportunity to walk my daughter down the aisle. It is a moment I have cherished in my heart for as long as I can remember—a moment that symbolizes the love and bond between a father and his daughter, speaks to the beauty of family, and will forever be etched in my memory.

To my beloved daughter, I offer these words of love and gratitude: Thank you for allowing me to be a part of this special day, for entrusting me with the honour of walking by your side as you begin this new chapter of your life. You have brought so much joy and love into my life, and I am profoundly grateful for the privilege of being your father.

As I walk you down the aisle today, know that my heart is overflowing with pride and love. You are a shining light in this world, a beacon of hope and inspiration to all who know you. May you continue to walk your path with grace and courage, knowing that you are loved beyond measure and supported unconditionally by all around you.

I extend my warmest welcome to my daughter's partner in our family. Today, as you stand beside my daughter, know that you are gaining a life partner and a cherished member of our family. I am grateful for the love and happiness you bring into my daughter's life, and I am excited to welcome you with open arms.

As we celebrate this joyous occasion, let us take a moment to express our gratitude for the love and support of our family and friends. Without their guidance and encouragement, we would not be here today, celebrating this beautiful union and embracing the promise of a future filled with love, laughter, and cherished memories.

To all who have gathered here today, I offer my heartfelt thanks for sharing in this special moment with us. Your presence fills our hearts with joy, and your love sustains us as we embark on this new journey together. May this day be a testament to the power of love to unite hearts and souls in a truly unbreakable bond.

As we prepare to take our first steps down the aisle together, let us cherish this moment and hold it in our hearts forever. Today, we celebrate not only the love that binds us together but also the love that will guide us on this incredible journey ahead.

Thank you, from the bottom of my heart.

***

"A Father's Reflection: The Timeless Bond Between Father and Daughter"

Ladies and gentlemen, esteemed family and friends,

As I stand before you today, surrounded by the love and warmth of our dear ones, I am humbled and deeply moved to reflect on the timeless bond between a father and his daughter. This bond, this sacred connection that transcends words and spans the passage of time, is one of life's greatest treasures—a bond forged in love, nurtured by moments of laughter and tears, and strengthened by the unbreakable ties of family.

From the moment my daughter entered this world, she captured my heart in a way I never knew possible. Her laughter became my melody, her smile my guiding light, and her presence my greatest joy. As I watched her take her first steps, utter her first words, and navigate the complexities of life with grace and resilience, I marvelled at the miracle of her existence and felt profoundly grateful for the privilege of being her father.

Through the years, we have shared countless moments together—moments of joy and celebration, moments of sadness and heartache, and moments of quiet reflection and shared understanding.

We have laughed together until our sides hurt, danced together under the stars, and held each other close in times of sorrow. And through it all, our bond has only grown stronger, deeper, and more unbreakable with each passing day.

For a father and daughter, there is a special kind of magic in the air—a magic that transcends the ordinary and transforms the mundane into moments of pure enchantment. It is the magic of shared secrets whispered in the dead of night, of inside jokes that need no explanation, and of knowing glances that speak volumes without a single word.

But perhaps the most beautiful aspect of the father-daughter bond is its capacity to evolve and adapt over time. From the tender innocence of childhood to the tumultuous years of adolescence and beyond, our relationship has weathered the storms of life with grace and resilience, emerging stronger and more resilient with each new challenge we face.

As I reflect on the journey that has brought us to this moment, I am filled with an overwhelming sense of gratitude—for the laughter that has echoed through our halls, for the tears that have been shed and wiped away, and for the countless memories that we have shared together. And as I look upon my daughter, radiant and resplendent on her wedding day, I am reminded of the incredible woman she has become—a woman of strength, courage, and boundless compassion.

Today, as I prepare to walk my daughter down the aisle and entrust her into the loving arms of her partner, I am filled with a myriad of emotions—joy, pride, and a hint of bittersweet nostalgia. For while I am thrilled to witness her embark on this new chapter of her life, a part of me will always long for the days when she was just a little girl, twirling around in her princess dress and dreaming of her happily ever after.

But as I take her hand in mine and guide her towards her future, I am filled with a profound sense of peace—a peace that comes from knowing that she is loved beyond measure, supported unconditionally, and cherished beyond words. For in her partner, I see not only a soulmate but also a kindred spirit—a partner who will stand by her side through life's ups and downs, who will lift her up when she falls, and who will love her with a depth and intensity that mirrors my own.

To my beloved daughter, I offer these words of love and wisdom: As you embark on this new journey with your partner, may you always remember the love that binds us together, the memories that sustain us, and the bond that will forever connect us, heart to heart. May you build a life filled with laughter, love, and shared dreams, and may you always know that you are loved beyond measure, cherished beyond words, and supported unconditionally by your father.

And to my daughter's partner, I extend my warmest welcome into our family. Today, as you join your life with hers, know that you are gaining a wife and a cherished daughter, sister, and friend. I am grateful for the love and happiness you bring into my daughter's life, and I am honoured to welcome you with open arms and an open heart.

As we celebrate this joyous occasion and bear witness to the union of two souls, let us take a moment to reflect on the beauty of the father-daughter bond—a bond that transcends time and space, and that will forever hold a special place in our hearts. Ultimately, the love we share, the memories we create, and the bonds we forge define us and sustain us on life's journey.

Thank you, from the bottom of my heart, for allowing me to reflect on the timeless bond between a father and his daughter. May our love shine brightly, lighting the way for all who follow in our footsteps, and may we always treasure the precious moments we share together, today and always.

***

"Sharing your hopes and dreams for her marriage"
Ladies and gentlemen, beloved family and friends,

As I stand before you today, surrounded by love and warmth, I am filled with profound emotion as I reflect on the hopes and dreams I hold for my daughter's marriage. This moment marks the beginning of a new chapter—a chapter filled with promise, adventure, and the boundless possibilities that come with building a life together.

From the day my daughter was born, I have held her in my arms and cherished every moment of her journey through life. I have watched her grow into the remarkable woman she is today—a woman of grace, compassion, and unwavering determination. And now, as she stands before us, radiant and resplendent on her wedding day, I am filled with an overwhelming sense of pride and joy.

To my beloved daughter and her partner, I offer these words of hope and encouragement: May your marriage be a journey of discovery—a journey filled with laughter, love, and shared dreams. May you always walk hand in hand, supporting each other through life's challenges and celebrating each triumph with joy and gratitude.

May you nurture your relationship with kindness and compassion, never losing sight of the love that brought you together. May you communicate openly and honestly, listening to each other's hopes, fears, and dreams with empathy and understanding. And may you always prioritize your relationship, making time for each other amidst life's many distractions and responsibilities.

As you navigate the highs and lows of marriage, may you remember the vows you have made to one another—to love, honour, and cherish each other, for better or for worse, for richer or for poorer, in sickness and in health, until death do you part. May you honour these vows not only in word but also in deed, showing each other the same love and respect that you wish to receive in return.

May your home be a sanctuary—a place of warmth, acceptance, and unconditional love. May you create a space where you can be your true selves, where you can laugh together, cry together, and grow together as individuals and as partners. And may you fill your home with laughter, music, and the simple pleasures that bring you joy.

As you build your life together, may you never lose sight of the importance of compromise, forgiveness, and patience. May you approach each day with a spirit of gratitude, recognizing the blessings that surround you and the beauty of the life you have created together. And may you face the future with courage and optimism, knowing that with love as your guide, there is nothing you cannot overcome.

To my daughter's partner, I extend my warmest welcome into our family. Today, as you join your life with hers, know that you are not only gaining a wife but also a cherished daughter, sister, and friend. I am grateful for the love and happiness you bring into my daughter's life, and I am honoured to welcome you with open arms and an open heart.

As we gather here today to celebrate this joyous occasion, let us take a moment to reflect on the beauty of love and the power of commitment. Let us celebrate the love that binds my daughter and her partner together—a love that is as enduring as it is profound, as beautiful as it is rare.

May your marriage be a beacon of hope and inspiration to all who know you—a testament to the transformative power of love and the beauty of two souls joined as one. And may your hearts be forever filled with the joy of each other's company, the warmth of each other's embrace, and the promise of a future filled with love, laughter, and endless possibilities.

Thank you, from the bottom of my heart, for allowing me to share my hopes and dreams for my daughter's marriage. May your love continue to grow stronger with each passing day, and may your bond be a source of strength and comfort as you journey through life together, hand in hand, heart to heart.

***

"Wisdom for a Lifelong Journey: A Father's Advice for a Strong and Lasting Marriage"

Ladies and gentlemen, esteemed family and friends,

As we gather here today to celebrate the union of two souls, I am deeply honoured to share with you some words of advice for a strong and lasting marriage. As the father of the bride, I have been blessed with the opportunity to witness the beauty of love and the power of commitment, and it is with great humility and gratitude that I offer these words of wisdom to my daughter and her partner as they embark on this incredible journey together.

First and foremost, I believe that communication is the cornerstone of a strong and healthy marriage. In any relationship, open and honest communication is essential for understanding, empathy, and mutual respect. Take the time to truly listen to each other, to share your thoughts, feelings, and dreams, and to approach every conversation with kindness and compassion. Remember that communication is not just about talking—it's also about truly hearing and understanding each other's perspectives.

Secondly, I encourage you to always prioritize your relationship and make time for each other amidst life's many demands and responsibilities. In the hustle and bustle of everyday life, it's easy to get caught up in work, chores, and other obligations, but it's essential to carve out quality time for each other. Whether it's a weekly date night, a leisurely walk in the park, or simply curling up on the couch together, make an effort to nurture your bond and strengthen your connection on a regular basis.

Furthermore, I urge you to approach challenges and conflicts with patience, understanding, and a spirit of compromise. Marriage is not always easy, and there will inevitably be times when you disagree or face difficult decisions together. In these moments, remember to approach each other with kindness and respect, to seek common ground, and to work together as a team to find solutions that benefit both of you.

Remember that you are not adversaries—you are partners, and together, you can overcome any obstacle that comes your way.

Moreover, I encourage you to always show appreciation and gratitude for each other's strengths, contributions, and efforts. In the hustle and bustle of everyday life, it's easy to take each other for granted, but it's essential to pause and acknowledge the love, support, and sacrifices that you both make for each other. Whether it's a simple thank you, a heartfelt gesture, or a kind word of encouragement, never underestimate the power of gratitude to strengthen your bond and deepen your connection.

In addition, I believe that it's crucial to maintain a sense of humour and light-heartedness in your marriage. Life is unpredictable, and there will inevitably be moments of stress, frustration, and disappointment. In these moments, don't be afraid to laugh together, to find joy in the little things, and to approach life with a sense of playfulness and spontaneity. Remember that laughter truly is the best medicine, and it can bring you closer together even in the face of adversity.

Furthermore, I encourage you to never stop growing and evolving as individuals and as a couple. Marriage is a journey of self-discovery, growth, and transformation, and it's essential to continue learning, exploring, and challenging yourselves both individually and together. Whether it's pursuing new hobbies, setting goals for the future, or embarking on new adventures, never lose sight of the potential for growth and development that lies within each of you.

Lastly, I believe that it's essential to always keep the flame of romance alive in your marriage. Never stop courting each other, surprising each other, and expressing your love and affection in meaningful ways. Whether it's a handwritten love note, a spontaneous gesture of affection, or a romantic getaway, never underestimate the power of romance to reignite the spark and keep your love burning brightly for years to come.

In closing, I offer these words of advice with the deepest love and respect for my daughter and her partner. May your marriage be a source of strength, joy, and inspiration—a partnership built on a foundation of love, trust, and mutual respect. May you continue to nurture your bond, cherish each other's presence, and grow stronger together with each passing day. And may your love continue to shine brightly, lighting the way for all who follow in your footsteps.

Thank you.

***

Ladies and gentlemen, esteemed family and friends,

As I stand before you today, my heart is filled with nostalgia and fond memories as I reminisce about my daughter's favourite childhood activities and hobbies. From the moment she came into this world, she was a bundle of joy and energy, eager to explore the world around her and discover new adventures at every turn.

One of my daughter's favourite childhood pastimes was spending hours immersed in the world of books. From the time she could hold a book in her tiny hands, she was captivated by the magic of storytelling, eagerly devouring every page and losing herself in the fantastical worlds that lay within. I can still picture her curled up in her favourite armchair, lost in a world of imagination, her eyes sparkling with wonder and delight.

Another beloved hobby of hers was painting and drawing. From a young age, she displayed a natural talent for art, creating colorful masterpieces that adorned our walls and filled our hearts with joy. Whether she was painting landscapes, sketching portraits, or experimenting with different mediums, her creativity knew no bounds, and her passion for art was truly infectious.

But perhaps my daughter's greatest love of all was music. From the first time she heard the strains of a melody, she was entranced by the beauty of sound and the power of music to stir the soul. Whether she was singing along to her favourite songs, playing the piano, or composing her own melodies, music was always a source of joy and inspiration for her—a way to express herself, connect with others, and find solace in times of need.

As I reflect on these cherished memories, I am filled with gratitude for the precious moments we shared together. Whether we were reading bedtime stories, creating art projects, or singing songs around the piano, each moment was a testament to the love and bond between a father and his daughter—a bond that remains unbreakable to this day.

As my daughter grew older, her interests and hobbies evolved, but her passion for learning, creativity, and self-expression never waned. She continued to explore new avenues of artistic expression, from photography to writing to dance, always eager to push the boundaries of her creativity and challenge herself to new heights.

Today, as I look upon my daughter on her wedding day, I am filled with pride and admiration for the incredible woman she has become. She has grown from a curious and adventurous child into a strong, confident, and compassionate adult—a woman who is not afraid to chase her dreams, stand up for what she believes in, and love with all her heart.

To my beloved daughter, I offer these words of encouragement and support: Never stop chasing your dreams, embracing your passions, and exploring the world around you. Remember that life is a journey filled with endless possibilities, and that anything is possible with hard work, determination, and a generous dose of creativity. Know that you are loved beyond measure, supported unconditionally, and cherished beyond words, and that no matter where life may take you, you will always have a home in the hearts of those who love you.

And to my daughter's partner, I extend my warmest welcome into our family. Today, as you join your life with hers, know that you are gaining a wife and a cherished daughter, sister, and friend. I am grateful for the love and happiness you bring into my daughter's life, and I am honoured to welcome you with open arms and an open heart.

As we celebrate this joyous occasion and bear witness to the union of two souls, let us take a moment to reflect on the beauty of childhood memories and the power of shared experiences to shape our lives and our relationships. In the end, it is the love we share, the memories we create, and the bonds we forge that truly define us and sustain us on life's journey.

Thank you, from the bottom of my heart, for allowing me to remember my daughter's favourite childhood activities and hobbies. May these cherished memories continue to bring us joy and inspiration for years to come, and may we always treasure the precious moments we share, today and always.

***

"Shared Laughter, Unforgettable Memories: A Father's Reflections on Inside Jokes with His Daughter"

Ladies and gentlemen, cherished family and friends,

Today, as I stand before you to celebrate the union of two souls, I am filled with joy, nostalgia, and a hint of mischief as I reflect on the countless inside jokes and funny anecdotes that my daughter and I have shared over the years. These moments of laughter and connection have been a constant source of joy and comfort, serving as a reminder of the special bond that exists between a father and his daughter. This bond transcends time and space and is forged in the fires of shared experiences and cherished memories.

One of our favourite inside jokes revolves around a family vacation many years ago. We were exploring a new city, and my daughter, ever the adventurous spirit, insisted on trying out the local cuisine. Little did we know that her adventurous palate would lead us on a culinary adventure we would never forget! From sampling exotic dishes to attempting to pronounce unfamiliar menu items, we found ourselves in fits of laughter at our culinary misadventures. This shared experience still brings a smile to our faces to this day.

Another cherished memory that always brings a chuckle is when my daughter decided to surprise me with breakfast in bed on Father's Day. Bless her heart, she had the best intentions, but let's say her culinary skills were still a work in progress at the time! I'll never forget the look of determination on her face as she presented me with a plate of burnt toast and scrambled eggs that were a tad bit too runny. Despite the less-than-perfect meal, it was one of the most delicious breakfasts I've ever had, simply because it was made with love.

And then there was the time when my daughter decided to teach me how to dance. Now, I'll be the first to admit that I'm not exactly the most graceful dancer, but she insisted on giving me a crash course in boogieing down. Suffice it to say; hilarity ensued as we tripped over each other's feet, spun in circles, and attempted to master the intricate steps of her favourite dance moves. It may not have been a perfect performance, but it was certainly a memorable one—a shared moment of laughter and joy that I will treasure forever.

Of course, no collection of inside jokes would be complete without mentioning our beloved family pet—a mischievous little furball who never failed to keep us on our toes. From stealing socks to chasing imaginary squirrels, he gave us endless entertainment and countless moments of laughter. One of our favourite memories is the time he decided to "help" with the gardening by digging up the flower beds and proudly presenting us with his latest treasures—a collection of shoes, toys, and assorted household items that he had buried in the backyard. It was a classic case of doggie mischief that still makes us laugh to this day.

But perhaps the greatest inside joke of all is the one that needs no words—the silent understanding that comes from a shared glance, a knowing smile, or a simple gesture that speaks volumes. It's the way we can communicate without saying a word, the way we can finish each other's sentences, and the way we can laugh together at the most mundane of things. It's a bond that transcends language and defies explanation—a connection only a father and his daughter can truly understand.

As I look upon my daughter on her wedding day, I am filled with an overwhelming sense of gratitude for the countless moments of laughter and love that we have shared. From inside jokes to shared adventures, our bond is unbreakable—a testament to the power of love, laughter, and the special connection between a father and his daughter.

To my beloved daughter, I offer these words of love and gratitude: Thank you for filling my life with laughter, love, and countless memories that I will treasure forever. You are my greatest joy, my proudest achievement, and my closest confidante, and I am eternally grateful for the privilege of being your father.

And to my daughter's partner, I extend my warmest welcome to our family. Today, as you join your life with hers, know that you are gaining a wife and a cherished daughter, sister, and friend. I am grateful for the love and happiness you bring into my daughter's life, and I am honoured to welcome you with open arms and an open heart.

As we celebrate this joyous occasion and bear witness to the union of two souls, let us take a moment to reflect on the beauty of shared laughter and the power of inside jokes to strengthen our bonds and deepen our connections. For in the end, it is the love we share, the memories we create, and the laughter we share together that truly define us and sustain us on life's journey.

Thank you, from the bottom of my heart, for allowing me to reflect on the countless inside jokes and funny anecdotes my daughter and I have shared over the years. May these cherished memories continue to bring us laughter and joy for many years to come, and may our bond remain as strong and unbreakable as ever.

***

"A Daughter's Heart of Gold: A Father's Gratitude"

Ladies and gentlemen, beloved family and friends,

Today, as I stand before you with a heart full of gratitude and pride, I am compelled to express my deepest appreciation for my daughter's kindness, compassion, and generosity. Throughout her life, she has embodied these qualities in everything she does, touching the lives of those around her with her gentle spirit, selfless acts, and unwavering love.

From a young age, my daughter has possessed a heart of gold—a heart that overflows with compassion and empathy for others. Whether it's lending a listening ear to a friend in need, volunteering her time to help those less fortunate, or simply offering a kind word or a warm smile to brighten someone's day, she has always gone out of her way to make a difference in the lives of others.

Her kindness knows no bounds, and she has a natural ability to see the good in everyone she meets. She treats each person she encounters with respect, dignity, and understanding, recognizing every individual's inherent value and worth. Whether it's a stranger on the street or a loved one in need, she extends a hand of friendship and support, embodying the true meaning of compassion and empathy.

But perhaps what I admire most about my daughter is her generosity of spirit—a generosity that knows no limits and knows no bounds. She gives of herself freely and unconditionally, always willing to lend a helping hand, share her resources, and give back to those in need. Whether it's donating her time, money, or talents to charitable causes, she embodies the spirit of generosity in everything she does, inspiring those around her to do the same.

As her father, I am humbled and honoured to witness the impact of her kindness, compassion, and generosity on the world around her. She has touched the lives of so many people in so many ways, leaving a lasting legacy of love and compassion that will endure for generations to come.

To my beloved daughter, I offer these words of love and gratitude: Thank you for being the kind, compassionate, and generous soul that you are. Your kindness brightens the lives of everyone you meet, your compassion brings comfort to those in need, and your generosity inspires us all to be better versions of ourselves. You are a shining example of the power of love and compassion to make the world a better place, and I am eternally grateful for the privilege of being your father.

And to my daughter's partner, I extend my warmest welcome into our family. Today, as you join your life with hers, know that you are gaining a wife and a cherished daughter, sister, and friend. I am grateful for the love and happiness you bring into my daughter's life, and I am honoured to welcome you with open arms and an open heart.

As we celebrate this joyous occasion and bear witness to the union of two souls, let us take a moment to reflect on the beauty of kindness, compassion, and generosity. For in the end, it is these qualities that truly define us and sustain us on life's journey, and it is these qualities that make my daughter the extraordinary woman she is today.

Thank you, from the bottom of my heart, for allowing me to express my appreciation for my daughter's kindness, compassion, and generosity. May her love continue to shine brightly, lighting the way for all who follow in her footsteps, and may her legacy of love and compassion endure for generations to come.

***

"A Reflection on Values: A Father's Pride"

As I stand here today, watching my daughter embark on this beautiful journey of marriage, I can't help but reflect on the values and lessons that I've tried to instil in her over the years. From the moment she was born, I made a promise to myself to nurture her, guide her, and teach her the importance of kindness, integrity, and resilience.

One of the values that I've always tried to impart upon my daughter is the importance of kindness. I've encouraged her to treat others with compassion and empathy, to lend a helping hand to those in need, and to always strive to make the world a better place. Whether it's through simple acts of kindness or larger gestures of generosity, I've watched with pride as she has embraced the value of kindness and made it an integral part of who she is.

Another lesson that I've worked hard to teach my daughter is the importance of integrity. I've encouraged her to always be true to herself, to stand up for what she believes in, and to never compromise her values for the sake of fitting in or pleasing others. I've watched her navigate life with honesty and integrity, facing challenges with courage and grace, and always staying true to the principles that guide her.

Lastly, I've tried to instil in my daughter the value of resilience. Life is full of ups and downs, twists and turns, but it's how we respond to adversity that truly defines us. I've encouraged my daughter to face challenges head-on, to learn from her mistakes, and to never give up on her dreams. I've watched her overcome obstacles with strength and determination, emerging stronger and more resilient with each new challenge she faces.

As I look upon my daughter on her wedding day, I am filled with pride and gratitude. She has grown into a remarkable woman—a woman of kindness, integrity, and resilience—a woman who embodies the values that I've tried to instil in her from a young age. And as she embarks on this new chapter of her life, I do not doubt that she will continue to embrace these values and live her life with purpose, passion, and compassion.

To my beloved daughter, I offer these words of love and encouragement: Continue to embrace the values that have guided you thus far—kindness, integrity, and resilience. They are the foundation upon which you have built your life and will continue to sustain you on your journey. Know that you are loved beyond measure, supported unconditionally, and cherished beyond words, and that no matter where life may take you, you will always have a home in the hearts of those who love you.

Thank you, from the bottom of my heart, for allowing me to reflect on the values and lessons I've tried to instil in my daughter. May they continue to guide, inspire, and shape her into the extraordinary woman she is destined to be.

***

"A Journey of Beauty and Joy: Reflecting on My Daughter's Growth into Womanhood"

Ladies and gentlemen, esteemed family and friends,

Today, as I stand before you with a heart full of pride and gratitude, I am moved to reflect on the incredible journey of watching my daughter grow into the remarkable woman she is today. From the moment she came into this world, she has been a source of endless beauty, joy, and inspiration—a shining light in my life and in the lives of all who know her.

As I look back on the years that have passed, I am filled with awe and wonder at the incredible transformation my daughter has undergone—from a curious and carefree child to a confident and compassionate woman. It has been a privilege to witness her growth and evolution, to stand by her side as she navigated the challenges of adolescence and emerged stronger, wiser, and more resilient than ever before.

One of the most beautiful aspects of watching my daughter grow into womanhood has been witnessing her embrace her own unique beauty and strength. From a young age, she has possessed an inner radiance and grace that have captivated everyone she meets. Whether it's her infectious laughter, her warm smile, or the sparkle in her eyes, she has a beauty that radiates from within—a beauty that is as timeless as it is captivating.

But beyond her physical beauty, it is my daughter's inner strength and resilience that truly inspire me. She has faced challenges with grace and courage, overcoming obstacles with determination and perseverance. From navigating the trials and tribulations of school to overcoming personal setbacks and disappointments, she has demonstrated a resilience and strength of character that are truly awe-inspiring.

Moreover, I have been privileged to witness my daughter's unwavering commitment to kindness, compassion, and generosity. She has a heart as big as the sky, always willing to lend a helping hand, offer a listening ear, or share a kind word of encouragement. Whether it's volunteering her time to help those in need, standing up for what she believes in, or simply spreading love and positivity wherever she goes, she embodies the true essence of compassion and empathy.

As I reflect on the beauty and joy of watching my daughter grow into a woman, I am filled with an overwhelming sense of gratitude for the privilege of being her father. She has brought so much love, laughter, and light into my life, and I am eternally grateful for every moment we have shared.

To my beloved daughter, I offer these words of love and encouragement: Continue to embrace the beauty and strength within you. You are a shining example of grace, resilience, and compassion, and I am so proud to be your father. As you embark on this new chapter of your life, know that you are loved beyond measure, supported unconditionally, and cherished beyond words.

And to my daughter's partner, I extend my warmest welcome into our family. Today, as you join your life with hers, know that you are gaining a wife and a cherished daughter, sister, and friend. I am grateful for the love and happiness you bring into my daughter's life, and I am honoured to welcome you with open arms and an open heart.

As we celebrate this joyous occasion and bear witness to the union of two souls, let us take a moment to reflect on the beauty and joy of watching my daughter grow into a woman. In the end, it is the love we share, the memories we create, and the bonds we forge that truly define us and sustain us on life's journey.

Thank you, from the bottom of my heart, for allowing me to reflect on the beauty and joy of watching my daughter grow into a woman. May her journey continue to be filled with love, laughter, and endless possibilities, and may her light continue to shine brightly for all the world to see.

***

"A Father's Wishes: Happiness and Fulfilment in Marriage"

Ladies and gentlemen, beloved family and friends,

As we gather here today to celebrate the union of two souls, I am filled with a profound sense of hope and anticipation for my daughter's happiness and fulfilment in marriage. From the moment she was born, my greatest wish has been for her to find love, joy, and fulfilment in all aspects of her life. And today, as she embarks on this new chapter with the love of her life by her side, I am filled with hope and optimism for the beautiful journey that lies ahead.

To my beloved daughter and her partner, I offer these heartfelt wishes:

May your marriage be a sanctuary—a place of love, laughter, and endless possibilities. May you create a home filled with warmth, acceptance, and unconditional love, where you can be your true selves and find solace in each other's embrace.

May your partnership be a source of strength and support, guiding you through life's challenges and celebrating each triumph with joy and gratitude. May you face the ups and downs of life together, hand in hand, heart to heart, knowing that you are stronger together than you could ever be apart.

May your love continue to grow stronger with each passing day, deepening and evolving as you journey through life together. May you never lose sight of the magic and wonder of love, and may you always cherish the bond that unites you in heart and soul.

May you communicate openly and honestly, listening to each other's hopes, fears, and dreams with empathy and understanding. May you always strive to be each other's greatest champion, supporting and encouraging one another to reach for the stars and pursue your dreams with passion and determination.

May you never forget the importance of laughter, playfulness, and spontaneity in your marriage. May you find joy in the simple moments—the shared meals, the quiet walks, the late-night conversations—and may you always take the time to nurture your bond and strengthen your connection.

And above all, may your marriage be a reflection of the love, commitment, and devotion that you share for one another. May you honour your vows not only in word but also in deed, showing each other the same love, respect, and kindness that you wish to receive in return.

To my daughter and her partner, I offer these wishes with all the love and hope in my heart. May your marriage be a journey of love, growth, and endless possibilities, and may you find happiness and fulfilment in each other's arms, today and always.

Thank you, from the bottom of my heart, for allowing me the privilege of sharing my hopes and wishes for my daughter's happiness and fulfilment in marriage. May your love continue to blossom and flourish, lighting the way for all who know you and bringing joy and inspiration to all who witness your beautiful union.

***

"Gratitude for a Lifetime of Love: A Father's Tribute"

Ladies and gentlemen, cherished family and friends,

Today, as we celebrate the union of two hearts, I am filled with an overwhelming sense of gratitude for the love and support my daughter has given me over the years. From the moment she entered my life, she has been a beacon of light, guiding me through the ups and downs with unwavering love, compassion, and understanding.

To my beloved daughter,

As I stand before you on this joyous occasion, I am filled with pride and gratitude for the incredible woman you have become. From the day you were born, you have brought so much love, joy, and laughter into my life, and I am eternally grateful for every moment we have shared together.

Thank you for being my rock, confidante, and greatest source of strength. Thank you for always believing in me, even when I doubted myself, and for standing by my side through thick and thin. Your love and support have been a constant source of comfort and inspiration, and I am truly blessed to have you as my daughter.

Thank you for teaching me the true meaning of unconditional love. Through your kindness, generosity, and compassion, you have shown me the beauty of selflessness and the power of love to heal, to transform, and to uplift. Your love has been a guiding light in my darkest moments, and I am forever grateful for the warmth and comfort it brings to my heart.

Thank you for the countless sacrifices you have made on my behalf. From the late nights spent studying for exams to the early mornings spent driving me to school or practice, you have always put my needs before your own, and for that, I am endlessly grateful. Your selflessness and devotion are a testament to the depth of your love, and your unwavering dedication to my happiness and well-being deeply humbles me.

Thank you for being my inspiration and my role model. Your strength, courage, and resilience in the face of adversity have taught me the true meaning of perseverance and determination. You have faced life's challenges with grace and dignity, never losing sight of the beauty and wonder that surround you, and I am in awe of your unwavering optimism and zest for life.

And most of all, thank you for being you—for your unique spirit, your boundless enthusiasm, and your infectious laughter that lights up the room. You are a shining star in my life, and I am grateful for every moment I get to spend in your presence.

As you embark on this new chapter of your life, know that my love for you knows no bounds. I am here for you always, cheering you on, supporting you, and loving you with all my heart. May your marriage be filled with love, laughter, and endless joy, and may you continue to inspire all who know you with your kindness, compassion, and grace.

Thank you, my dear daughter, for the gift of your love. You are truly the light of my life, and I am eternally grateful for the blessing of having you as my daughter.

With all my love and gratitude,

***

"A Tribute to Strength: Celebrating My Daughter's Resilience"

Ladies and gentlemen, esteemed family and friends,

Today marks a momentous occasion as we gather to celebrate the union of two souls, but amidst the joy and festivities, I find myself reflecting on the remarkable journey of my daughter—a journey defined by strength, resilience, and unwavering determination.

To my beloved daughter,

As I stand before you today, I am filled with an overwhelming sense of admiration for the incredible woman you have become. From the beginning, you have faced life's challenges with courage and grace, and your strength has inspired all who know you.

Thank you for your unwavering resilience in the face of adversity. You have encountered obstacles and setbacks throughout your life, but you have never allowed them to define you. Instead, you have risen above them, becoming stronger and more determined. Your resilience is a testament to your inner strength and determination, and I am in awe of your ability to face life's challenges with courage and grace.

Thank you for your unwavering determination to pursue your dreams. You have set ambitious goals for yourself from a young age and worked tirelessly to achieve them. Whether it's your academic pursuits, career aspirations, or personal goals, you have approached each challenge with a fierce determination and an unyielding resolve to succeed. Your determination is a testament to your tenacity and perseverance, and your relentless pursuit of excellence inspires me.

Thank you for your unwavering commitment to making a difference in the world. You have a heart as big as the sky, and your compassion and empathy know no bounds. Whether it's volunteering your time to help those in need, advocating for causes you believe in, or simply lending a listening ear to a friend in need, you are always there to offer support, comfort, and encouragement. Your compassion is a testament to your kindness and generosity of spirit, and your selflessness and dedication move me to making the world a better place.

As you embark on this new chapter of your life, know that your strength, resilience, and determination have prepared you well for the journey ahead. You are a force to be reckoned with—a woman of courage, grace, and unwavering resolve—and I do not doubt that you will continue to inspire all who know you with your strength and resilience.

May your marriage be filled with love, laughter, and endless joy, and may you continue to shine brightly, lighting the way for all who follow in your footsteps. You inspire me, and I am eternally grateful for the blessing of having you as my daughter.

With all my love and admiration,

***

"A Father's Joy: Witnessing My Daughter's Happiness"
Ladies and gentlemen, beloved family and friends,

Today, as we celebrate the union of two hearts, I am filled with an indescribable sense of joy and gratitude for the privilege of being my daughter's father and the sheer happiness that radiates from her being.

To my beloved daughter,

As I stand before you on this momentous occasion, I am filled with overwhelming pride and joy as I reflect on the incredible journey of watching you grow into the beautiful, confident, and radiant woman you are today. From the very moment you came into my life, you brought an abundance of love, laughter, and light that has enriched my life in ways I never thought possible.

Thank you for the countless moments of joy and laughter that you have brought into my life. From your infectious giggles as a child to your radiant smile as a woman, your happiness has been a constant source of joy and inspiration to me. Your zest for life, your unwavering optimism, and your ability to find joy in even the simplest of pleasures remind me every day of the beauty and wonder that surrounds us, and for that, I am eternally grateful.

Thank you for allowing me to witness your happiness and fulfilment as you embark on this new chapter of your life. Your eyes sparkle with excitement, your heart brims with love, and your smile shines with pure joy, illuminating the world around you with its warmth and radiance. Seeing you so happy and in love fills my heart with an indescribable sense of happiness and contentment, and I am filled with gratitude for the love and happiness that you have found.

Thank you for teaching me the true meaning of unconditional love and selflessness. From the moment you were born, my greatest joy has been to love and protect you, support and guide you, and be there for you through every triumph and trial. Your happiness has always been my greatest priority and seeing you so happy and fulfilled today fills my heart with an overwhelming sense of pride and gratitude.

As you embark on this new chapter of your life, know that my love for you knows no bounds. I am here for you always, cheering you on, supporting you, and loving you with all my heart. May your marriage be filled with love, laughter, and endless joy, and may you continue to shine brightly, lighting the way for all who know you.

Thank you, my dear daughter, for the gift of your happiness. You are truly the light of my life, and I am eternally grateful for the blessing of having you as my daughter.

With all my love and gratitude,

***

"A Father's Pride: Celebrating My Daughter's Achievements"

My Dearest Emily

As I write this letter, my heart is overflowing with pride and admiration for the incredible woman you have become. Since you entered this world, you have filled my life with joy, love, and boundless pride, and I am endlessly grateful for the privilege of being your father.

I want you to know how proud I am of all you have accomplished and achieved throughout your life. From your earliest days, you have demonstrated a remarkable determination, passion, and resilience that have propelled you to great heights and inspired all who know you. Whether it's your academic pursuits, career aspirations, or personal goals, you have approached each challenge with unwavering determination and an unyielding commitment to excellence.

I am proud of the incredible academic achievements you have accomplished. From your early days in school to your college and university years, you have consistently demonstrated a thirst for knowledge, a love of learning, and a dedication to academic excellence that have set you apart from your peers. Your hard work, dedication, and perseverance have been nothing short of inspiring, and I am endlessly proud of the academic honours and accolades you have received throughout your journey.

I am proud of the passion and creativity you bring to everything you do. Whether it's your artistic pursuits, entrepreneurial ventures, or community involvement, you approach each endeavour with enthusiasm, creativity, and a spirit of innovation that never fails to impress me. Your passion for life, your thirst for adventure, and your willingness to think outside the box are qualities that I admire deeply, and I am proud to see you pursue your dreams with courage and conviction.

I am proud of the kindness, compassion, and empathy you show to others. From your earliest days, you have possessed a generous spirit and a caring heart, always willing to lend a helping hand, offer a listening ear, or share a kind word of encouragement. Your empathy, compassion, and willingness to make a difference in the lives of others are qualities that I cherish deeply, and I am proud to see you use your gifts and talents to make the world a better place.

But above all, I am proud of the person you have become—the kind, compassionate, and courageous woman who stands before me today. Your strength, resilience, and unwavering commitment to your values and beliefs are qualities that I admire deeply, and I am honoured to call you my daughter.

As you embark on this new chapter of your life, I want you to know that my pride in you knows no bounds. You have accomplished so much already, and I do not doubt that you will continue to achieve great things in the future. Remember that no matter where life may take you, you will always have a loving father cheering you on, supporting you, and loving you with all his heart.

With all my love and pride,

**

"Navigating the Journey Together: A Father's Advice for Sammy on Married Life"

Dear Sammy,

As I write this letter to you, my heart is filled with joy and anticipation for the journey ahead for you and my beloved daughter. As you embark on this new chapter of your life together, I wanted to take a moment to offer you some words of advice and wisdom that I hope will serve you well as you navigate the ups and downs of married life.

First and foremost, always remember the importance of communication. Communication is the cornerstone of any successful relationship, and it is essential to open, honest, and respectful communication to build a strong and lasting marriage. Take the time to truly listen to one another, to express your thoughts and feelings openly and honestly, and to communicate your needs, desires, and concerns with compassion and understanding. Remember that communication is not just about talking, but also about actively listening and seeking to understand one another's perspectives.

Secondly, never lose sight of the importance of compromise and teamwork. Marriage is a partnership, and it requires a willingness to compromise, collaborate, and work together as a team to overcome challenges and achieve common goals. There will inevitably be times when you disagree or face obstacles, but how you navigate these challenges together will ultimately determine the strength of your relationship. Approach each situation with a spirit of cooperation and mutual respect, and always prioritize the well-being and happiness of your partnership above all else.

Next, don't be afraid to seek support and guidance when needed. Marriage is a journey filled with twists and turns, and there may be times when you feel overwhelmed or unsure of how to proceed. In those moments, remember that you are not alone. Lean on each other for support, seek guidance from trusted friends and family members, and don't hesitate to seek professional help if needed. There is no shame in asking for assistance; reaching out for support can strengthen your bond and help you navigate challenges more effectively.

Additionally, never underestimate the power of laughter and fun in your marriage. Life is too short to take things too seriously, and it's important to find joy and laughter in the everyday moments you share together. Make time for fun and laughter, embrace spontaneity and adventure, and never stop finding ways to make each other smile. Laughter brings people closer together and reminds us of the love and joy that fills our hearts, so never underestimate its importance in your relationship.

Finally, always remember to cherish and nurture the love you share. Marriage is a journey, not a destination, requiring ongoing effort, commitment, and dedication to thrive. Take the time to nurture your love, show appreciation and gratitude for one another, and celebrate your unique bond. Remember that love is not just a feeling, but also a choice—a choice to show up for one another, to support one another, and to cherish one another through all of life's ups and downs.

As you embark on this new chapter of your life together, know that you have my unconditional love and support. I am so proud of the man you have become, and I do not doubt that you will be an incredible husband to my daughter. May your marriage be filled with love, laughter, and endless joy, and may you navigate life's journey together with grace, resilience, and unwavering love.

With all my love and best wishes,

***

"Embracing New Beginnings: A Father's Reflections for Stacey on Her Wedding Day"

Dear Stacey,

Today, as you stand on the threshold of a new chapter, ready to embark on the journey of marriage with the love of your life by your side, I wanted to take a moment to share some reflections and words of wisdom that I hope will serve you well as you begin this new adventure.

First and foremost, I want to express my profound joy and gratitude for the privilege of being your father. From the moment you came into this world, you brought an abundance of love, light, and laughter into my life, and I am endlessly grateful for every moment we have shared. Watching you grow into the remarkable woman you are today has been one of the greatest joys of my life, and I am filled with pride and admiration for the incredible person you have become.

Today marks a significant milestone in your journey—a day filled with love, hope, and promise as you join your life with your partner's and embark on the adventure of marriage together. It is a day that will forever be etched in your memory—a day of love, laughter, and cherished moments with family and friends. But beyond the pomp and circumstance of the wedding day itself, it also marks the beginning of a new family—a family built on love, trust, and shared dreams.

As you stand before the altar, surrounded by your loved ones, I want you to take a moment to reflect on the significance of this day and the journey that lies ahead. Marriage is a sacred bond—a union of hearts, minds, and souls—and it is a commitment to love, honour, and cherish one another through all of life's joys and challenges. It is a journey of growth, discovery, and transformation—a journey that will test your patience, your resilience, and your capacity for love, but also a journey that will bring you immeasurable joy, fulfilment, and happiness.

As you embark on this new chapter of your life, I offer you these words of wisdom and guidance:

Firstly, cherish the love and companionship you share with your partner. Love is the foundation upon which your marriage is built, and it is the glue that will hold you together through the trials and tribulations of life. Nurture your love, prioritize each other's happiness, and never take the gift of love for granted.

Secondly, never lose sight of the importance of communication and compromise. Marriage requires open, honest, and respectful communication in order to thrive, and it requires a willingness to compromise, collaborate, and work together as a team. Approach each challenge with a spirit of cooperation and understanding, and always prioritize your partnership above all else.

Thirdly, remember to make time for each other and for the things that bring you joy. Life can be hectic and demanding, but it's important to carve out time for intimacy, connection, and shared experiences. Whether it's a romantic date night, a weekend getaway, or a simple evening spent cuddled up on the couch, make time to nurture your bond and strengthen your connection.

And finally, never underestimate the importance of laughter, forgiveness, and gratitude in your marriage. Laughter has a way of bringing people closer together, forgiveness has the power to heal even the deepest wounds, and gratitude can transform even the most challenging situations. Cultivate a spirit of laughter, forgiveness, and gratitude in your marriage, and you will find that your love will only continue to deepen and grow with each passing day.

As you begin this new chapter of your life, know that you have my unconditional love and support. I am so proud of the woman you have become, and I do not doubt that you will be an incredible wife and partner to your beloved. May your marriage be filled with love, laughter, and endless joy, and may you navigate life's journey together with grace, resilience, and unwavering love.

With all my love and best wishes,

***

"Embracing the Journey: A Father's Letter of Excitement for the Future"

My Dearest Stacey,

As I write this letter to you, my heart is filled with an overwhelming sense of joy and excitement for the journey ahead for you. Today, as you stand on the threshold of a new chapter in your life, ready to embark on the adventure of marriage with the love of your life by your side, I am filled with a multitude of emotions—pride, happiness, nostalgia, and a profound sense of anticipation for all the wonderful experiences and adventures that await you.

From the moment you were born, you brought an abundance of love, light, and laughter into my life, and watching you grow into the remarkable woman you are today has been one of the greatest joys of my life. You have always inspired me—a beacon of strength, resilience, and unwavering determination—and I am endlessly proud of the person you have become.

Today marks the beginning of a new chapter—a chapter filled with love, laughter, and cherished memories as you join your life with your partner's and embark on the adventure of marriage together. It is a day that will forever be etched in your memory—a day of joyous celebration, heartfelt vows, and cherished moments with family and friends. But beyond the excitement and anticipation of the wedding day itself, it is also a day that marks the beginning of a lifetime of love, growth, and shared experiences.

As you stand before the altar, surrounded by your loved ones, I want you to take a moment to reflect on the significance of this day and the journey that lies ahead. Marriage is a sacred bond—a union of hearts, minds, and souls—and it is a commitment to love, honour, and cherish one another through all of life's joys and challenges. It is a journey of growth, discovery, and transformation—a journey that will test your patience, your resilience, and your capacity for love, but also a journey that will bring you immeasurable joy, fulfilment, and happiness.

As you embark on this new chapter of your life, I offer you these words of wisdom and guidance:

Embrace the unknown with open arms and an adventurous spirit. Life is full of unexpected twists and turns, and it is the journey itself that is the greatest adventure of all. Embrace the unknown with courage, curiosity, and a sense of wonder, and don't be afraid to step outside your comfort zone and explore new horizons. Whether it's traveling to far-off destinations, pursuing new hobbies and interests, or taking on new challenges together, embrace the journey with open hearts and open minds, and allow yourselves to be swept away by the magic and beauty of life's adventures.

Cherish the moments of togetherness and connection. In the hustle and bustle of everyday life, it's easy to lose sight of the simple joys and pleasures that bring us closer together. Take the time to cherish the moments of togetherness and connection—the shared meals, the quiet evenings spent cuddled up on the couch, the laughter and joy of being in each other's company. These are the moments that create lasting memories and strengthen the bonds of love and affection that unite you as a couple, so cherish them dearly and hold them close to your hearts.

Celebrate each other's individuality and uniqueness. Marriage is a journey of growth and self-discovery, and it's important to honour and celebrate each other's individuality and uniqueness. Embrace the differences that make you both unique, celebrate each other's strengths and talents, and support each other's dreams and aspirations. Remember that you are partners in life, but you are also individuals with your own hopes, dreams, and desires, so encourage each other to pursue your passions and be true to yourselves.

And finally, never lose sight of the love and commitment that brought you together in the first place. Love is the foundation upon which your marriage is built, and the bond will sustain you through all of life's joys and challenges. Nurture your love, prioritize each other's happiness, and never take the gift of love for granted. Remember that love is not just a feeling, but also a choice—a choice to show up for one another, to support one another, and to cherish one another through all of life's ups and downs.

As you embark on this new chapter of your life, know that you have my unconditional love and support. I am so proud of the woman you have become, and I do not doubt that you will be an incredible wife and partner to your beloved. May your marriage be filled with love, laughter, and endless joy, and may you embrace each new day with open hearts and open minds, ready to embark on the adventure of a lifetime together.

With all my love and best wishes,

***

"Always by Your Side: A Father's Reassurance for Ella"

My Dearest Ella,

As I reflect on the beautiful journey of your life, one particular moment stands out vividly in my memory—an anecdote that I hold dear to my heart and one that I hope will offer you the reassurance and comfort you deserve as you embark on this new chapter of your life.

I remember a chilly autumn evening many years ago when you were just a little girl, barely tall enough to reach my knee. We were out for a walk in the park, the crunch of fallen leaves beneath our feet and the crispness of the air making everything feel alive with possibility. As we strolled along, hand in hand, you suddenly stopped in your tracks, a look of concern furrowing your brow.

"Daddy," you asked, your voice filled with worry, "what if I get lost?"

I knelt down beside you, my heart swelling with love and tenderness as I looked into your eyes, so full of innocence and trust. "Oh, my darling Ella," I whispered, gently brushing a lock of hair from your forehead, "even if you wander off the beaten path, even if you lose your way in the darkness of the night, know that I will always be there to guide you home."

In that moment, as I held you close in my arms, I made a silent promise to you—a promise to always be there for you, no matter what. A promise to be your beacon of light in the darkest of nights, your anchor in the stormiest of seas, your unwavering source of love and support through all of life's joys and challenges.

And now, as you stand before me on the threshold of a new chapter in your life, ready to embark on the adventure of marriage with the love of your life by your side, I want you to know that this promise still holds true. No matter where life may take you, no matter what trials and tribulations you may face, know that I will always be there for you—cheering you on, supporting you, and loving you with all my heart.

As you navigate the ups and downs of married life, remember that you are never alone. Lean on your partner for support, seek guidance from trusted friends and family members, but always remember that your father is here for you, ready to offer a listening ear, a shoulder to cry on, or a hand to hold whenever you need it most.

So, my dear Ella, as you embark on this new chapter of your life, know that you have my unwavering love and support. May your marriage be filled with love, laughter, and endless joy, and may you always find comfort and reassurance in the knowledge that your father will always be there for you, no matter what.

With all my love and best wishes,

***

"A Legacy of Love: Reflecting on Generations of Support for Ava"

My Dearest Ava,

As I sit down to write this letter to you, my mind drifts back to a cherished memory from my own childhood—a memory that continues to shape and inspire me to this day. It's a memory of love, support, and unwavering encouragement from my own parents, and it's a memory that I hold dear to my heart as I reflect on the journey that lies ahead for you.

I remember a time many years ago, when I was just a young boy, filled with hopes and dreams and a heart full of wonder. It was a particularly challenging period in my life, a time when I felt lost and uncertain about the path ahead. Yet, through it all, there was one constant—a source of unwavering love and support that never wavered, never faltered, never doubted my ability to overcome any obstacle that stood in my way.

It was the love of my own parents, Ava—your grandparents—who stood by my side through thick and thin, offering words of encouragement, guidance, and support that helped shape me into the person I am today. They believed in me when I doubted myself, they lifted me up when I stumbled, and they showed me the true meaning of unconditional love and support.

I remember countless moments spent in their embrace—late-night conversations filled with wisdom and laughter, quiet moments of reflection and contemplation, and cherished memories that I will carry with me always. They taught me the importance of kindness, compassion, and empathy, and they instilled in me a sense of resilience, determination, and unwavering faith in myself and my abilities.

As I look back on those formative years, I am filled with gratitude for the love and support of my own parents, and I am reminded of the profound impact that their guidance and encouragement have had on my life. They were my rock, my anchor, my guiding light in the stormiest of seas, and I am eternally grateful for the love and support they have shown me throughout the years.

And now, as you stand before me on the brink of a new chapter in your own life, ready to embark on the adventure of marriage with the love of your life by your side, I want you to know that you, too, have a legacy of love and support that stretches back through generations. You have the love and wisdom of your grandparents flowing through your veins, and you carry with you the strength, resilience, and unwavering determination that they have instilled in you since the day you were born.

As you navigate the ups and downs of married life, remember the love and support of your own parents and grandparents, and draw strength from the knowledge that you are never alone. Lean on your partner for support and seek guidance from trusted friends and family members, but always remember that you come from a long line of strong, resilient, and loving individuals who believe in you and your ability to overcome any challenge that comes your way.

So, my dear Ava, as you embark on this new chapter of your life, know that you have the love and support of your family behind you every step of the way. May your marriage be filled with love, laughter, and endless joy, and may you always find comfort and reassurance in the knowledge that you come from a legacy of love that will carry you through even the darkest of days.

With all my love and best wishes,

***

"Gratitude for Unconditional Love: A Father's Tribute to Christine"

My Dearest Christine,

As I reflect on the beautiful journey of your life, one particular memory stands out—a poignant moment that has left an indelible mark on my heart and serves as a testament to the depth of your love and forgiveness.

It was a difficult time in our lives, Christine—a time filled with tension, misunderstandings, and hurt feelings. I had made a mistake, a decision that I deeply regretted, and it had caused a rift between us that seemed impossible to mend. I remember the weight of guilt and shame that I carried in my heart, knowing that I had let you down and fearing that I had irreparably damaged our relationship.

But in the midst of my despair, you showed me a kindness and compassion that I will never forget. You looked past my mistakes and shortcomings and offered me the most precious gift of all—your forgiveness. You embraced me with open arms, wiped away my tears, and reminded me that love has the power to heal even the deepest wounds.

I remember the moment vividly, Christine—the moment when you reached out to me with a heart full of love and forgiveness, and I realized just how fortunate I was to have you as my daughter. In that moment, you taught me the true meaning of unconditional love—the kind of love that sees past our flaws and imperfections, the kind of love that forgives without reservation, the kind of love that binds us together even in the darkest of times.

Your love and forgiveness have been a guiding light in my life, Christine, and I am endlessly grateful for the grace and compassion you have shown me. You have taught me the importance of humility, empathy, and understanding, and you have reminded me that even in our darkest moments, love has the power to heal, transform, and uplift.

As you embark on this new chapter of your life, Christine, I want you to know how grateful I am for your love and forgiveness. May your marriage be filled with the same kindness, compassion, and understanding that you have shown me, and may you continue to inspire all who know you with your boundless capacity for love and forgiveness.

With all my love and gratitude,

***

"A Legacy of Love: Hopes for Future Generations - A Letter to Jasmin"
My Dearest Jasmin,

As I sit down to write this letter to you, my heart swells with love and pride for the incredible woman you have become. As your father, I have had the privilege of watching you grow, learn, and blossom into the remarkable individual you are today. And as I reflect on your journey, I am filled with hope and optimism for the future—both yours and that of future generations.

There is one particular memory that comes to mind—a cherished moment from your childhood that has stayed with me through the years. It was a warm summer evening, and we were sitting in the backyard, watching the stars twinkle in the night sky. You looked up at me with those big, curious eyes of yours and asked me a question that caught me off guard: "Daddy, what do you hope for me and my children someday?"

In that moment, as I looked into your innocent eyes, I felt a surge of emotion wash over me. I realized that my hopes and dreams for you were not just for your own happiness and fulfilment, but for the happiness and fulfilment of future generations—to create a legacy of love, kindness, and compassion that would endure long after we are gone.

I hope for a world where your children and grandchildren can grow up in a society that values empathy, understanding, and acceptance—a world where diversity is celebrated, differences are embraced, and everyone is treated with dignity and respect.

I hope for a world where your children and grandchildren can pursue their dreams and passions without fear or limitations—a world where opportunities are plentiful, barriers are dismantled, and every individual has the chance to thrive and succeed.

I hope for a world where your children and grandchildren can experience the wonders of nature and the beauty of our planet—a world where clean air, clean water, and abundant natural resources are protected and preserved for future generations to enjoy.

But above all, Jasmin, I hope for a world filled with love—a world where your children and grandchildren are surrounded by love, nurtured by love, and inspired by love. Love has the power to heal, to unite, and to transform, and it is my deepest hope that your family will be guided by love in all that they do.

As you embark on this new chapter of your life, Jasmin, I want you to know that you have the power to shape the future—to create a more just, compassionate, and loving world than the one we know today. And as your father, I will always be here to support you, to encourage you, and to cheer you on every step of the way.

May your journey be filled with love, laughter, and endless joy, and may you continue to inspire all who know you with your boundless spirit and unwavering determination.

With all my love and hopes for the future,

***

"Gratitude Across Families: A Father's Appreciation for Isla's Partner's Family"

Ladies and gentlemen, beloved family and friends,

As we gather here today to celebrate the union of two hearts, I am filled with an overwhelming sense of gratitude for the love and support that surrounds us, not only from our own family but also from the family of Isla's beloved partner. Today, I would like to take a moment to express my heartfelt thanks to each and every member of Isla's partner's family for the warmth, kindness, and generosity they have shown to Isla and our entire family.

From the moment Isla introduced us to her partner, we were welcomed into their family with open arms and open hearts. We were embraced as one of their own, invited into their homes, and treated with the same love and respect that they would offer to their own kin. Their love and acceptance have been a source of comfort and strength for Isla, and for that, we are eternally grateful.

I am deeply touched by the genuine warmth and hospitality that Isla's partner's family has extended to us, and I am humbled by the depth of their generosity and kindness. Whether it's a warm smile, a heartfelt conversation, or a helping hand in times of need, they have always been there for us, offering their unwavering support and encouragement every step of the way.

I am grateful for the sense of belonging and inclusion that Isla's partner's family has made us feel. They have welcomed us into their family gatherings, celebrated our milestones with us, and stood by our side through life's ups and downs. They have become an integral part of our lives, and I am deeply thankful for the love and friendship that they have brought into our lives.

I am also thankful for the beautiful example of love and unity that Isla's partner's family has set for us. Their bond is a testament to the power of love to transcend boundaries and bring people together, and I am inspired by the strength of their connection and the depth of their commitment to one another. They have shown us what it means to love unconditionally, to support one another wholeheartedly, and to embrace each other's differences with grace and humility.

As we come together to celebrate this joyous occasion, I want to express my deepest thanks to Isla's partner's family for the love, support, and friendship they have shown to us. You have enriched our lives in countless ways, and we are truly blessed to have you as part of our extended family. May our bonds of friendship and love continue to grow stronger with each passing day, and may we always cherish the special connection that unites us as one big, loving family.

To Isla's partner's family, thank you from the bottom of my heart for your love, your kindness, and your unwavering support. You have touched our lives in ways that words cannot express, and we are forever grateful for the gift of your friendship and the warmth of your love.

With deepest gratitude and warmest regards,

***

"Forever Yours: A Father's Enduring Love for Rachel"

Ladies and gentlemen, esteemed guests,

As I stand before you today, my heart is filled with an overwhelming sense of love and gratitude as I have the honour of speaking about my beloved daughter, Rachel. Rachel, my dear daughter, from the moment you came into my life, you have brought an abundance of joy, love, and light into my world. Today, as you stand before us, radiant and beautiful, ready to embark on the journey of marriage with the love of your life by your side, I want to take a moment to express the depth of my love and devotion to you, now and always.

Rachel, you have been the light of my life since the day you were born. From your earliest days, you captured my heart with your infectious laughter, your sparkling eyes, and your boundless curiosity about the world around you. You were always a source of joy and inspiration to me, filling our home with warmth and love with your presence.

As you grew from a spirited child into a remarkable woman, I watched in awe as you embraced life with courage, determination, and grace. You faced challenges head-on, never allowing setbacks to dampen your spirit or dim your light. You pursued your dreams with unwavering determination, always striving to be the best version of yourself, and you never lost sight of the values and principles that guide you.

Rachel, you have grown into a woman of strength, integrity, and compassion—a woman who brings light and love wherever you go. Your kindness, your generosity, and your unwavering compassion for others are qualities that I admire deeply, and I am endlessly proud of the person you have become.

Today, as I stand here before you, Rachel, I want you to know that my love for you knows no bounds. I love you more deeply than words can express, and I am grateful for every moment that we have shared together as father and daughter. You are the heart and soul of our family, and I am blessed beyond measure to call you my daughter.

As you embark on this new chapter of your life, Rachel, with your beloved partner by your side, I want you to know that my love and support will always be with you. No matter where life may take you, no matter what challenges you may face, I will always be here for you, cheering you on, supporting you, and loving you with all my heart.

May your marriage be filled with love, laughter, and endless joy, and may you continue to shine brightly, illuminating the lives of all who know you with your radiant spirit and unwavering love.

Rachel, my dear daughter, know that you are cherished beyond measure, and that my love for you will endure for all eternity.

With all my love and devotion,

Chapter 4 – Father of the Bride: Punny Words of Wisdom

1. "I'm not losing a daughter; I'm gaining a son-in-law—talk about a great exchange rate!"
2. "My daughter's wedding is like a good book: it has a great beginning, a memorable middle, and I can't wait to see how it ends!"
3. "As the father of the bride, I'm just here to give my daughter away... and maybe a few dad jokes too!"
4. "To the bride and groom: May your marriage be as long and happy as the line at the open bar!"
5. "Walking my daughter down the aisle? More like walking her down memory lane!"
6. "They say marriage is a three-ring circus: engagement ring, wedding ring, and suffering. Just kidding...mostly."
7. "My daughter's wedding is like a fine wine—it gets better with age, and I'm just here to toast to it!"
8. "My daughter found her lobster—now she's off to start her own 'Friends' spinoff!"
9. "To the happy couple: May your love be as everlasting as the line for cake at the reception!"
10. "I always knew my daughter would find someone special. Little did I know it would be someone who would take her off my hands!"
11. "To the bride and groom: May your love be stronger than your WiFi signal and your fridge always be full of food!"
12. "As the father of the bride, I have two words of advice: 'Yes, dear.'"
13. "To the bride and groom: May your love be like a fart—silent but deadly!"

14. "Walking my daughter down the aisle is like watching my favourite movie: I'm sad it's ending, but I'm excited about the sequel!"

15. "My daughter's wedding is like a good dessert: sweet, memorable, and I can't wait to have seconds!"

16. "They say a wedding is like a full-time job. Luckily, I've been preparing for overtime my whole life!"

17. "To the newlyweds: May your love be as strong as your WiFi signal and your patience as endless as your Netflix queue!"

18. "Walking my daughter down the aisle? It's like being the opening act for the main event!"

19. "My daughter's wedding is like a great song: it's got a catchy melody, heartfelt lyrics, and I'm the proud backup dancer!"

20. "To the bride and groom: May your love be as enduring as my jokes and your happiness as abundant as the wedding cake!"

21. "My daughter's wedding is like a pizza: it's cheesy, saucy, and I just can't get enough of it!"

22. "Walking my daughter down the aisle is like walking on air—except it's a lot more emotional and there's no safety net!"

23. "To the happy couple: May your marriage be as blissful as the honeymoon and your bank account as full as the wedding registry!"

24. "My daughter's wedding is like a good book: it's filled with laughter and tears, and I can't wait to see how the story unfolds!"

25. "To the bride and groom: May your love be like a fine wine—getting better with age and leaving you with a great hangover in the morning!"

These puns can add a touch of humour and warmth to the father of the bride's speech at a wedding, making it a memorable and enjoyable moment for everyone involved!

Chapter 5 – Anecdote Stories

1. The time your daughter tried to teach you a new dance move and ended up laughing so hard you both fell over.
2. The family road trip where your daughter insisted on being the navigator and led you to an unexpected adventure.
3. The first time your daughter rode a bike without training wheels, and you cheered her on from the sidelines.
4. The time your daughter surprised you with breakfast in bed on Father's Day and ended up making a mess in the kitchen.
5. The family camping trip where your daughter bravely caught her first fish and proudly showed it off to everyone.
6. The time your daughter performed in her school play, and you were so proud you couldn't stop beaming from the audience.
7. The family game night where your daughter invented her own set of rules and somehow managed to win every game.
8. The time your daughter rescued a stray kitten from the street and convinced you to let her keep it as a pet.
9. The day your daughter got her driver's license and took you for a nerve-wracking spin around the neighbourhood.
10. The family holiday where your daughter insisted on making her famous chocolate chip cookies for everyone to enjoy.
11. The time your daughter organized a surprise birthday party for you and invited all your friends and family.
12. The family tradition of baking cookies together every Christmas and the hilarious mishaps that ensued in the kitchen.
13. The time your daughter wrote you a heartfelt letter expressing her gratitude for everything you've done for her.
14. The family movie night where your daughter picked out a classic film and insisted on providing a running commentary throughout.

15. The day your daughter graduated from college, and you couldn't help but shed a tear of pride.

16. The time your daughter convinced you to try a new hobby together and you ended up having a blast.

17. The family camping trip where your daughter bravely faced her fear of heights and conquered the climbing wall.

18. The time your daughter surprised you with tickets to your favourite sports game and you bonded over cheering for your team.

19. The family tradition of Sunday morning pancake breakfasts and the competitive pancake-flipping contests that ensued.

20. The time your daughter taught you how to use social media and you accidentally posted embarrassing selfies for all to see.

21. The family vacation where your daughter insisted on documenting every moment with her camera and created a hilarious photo album.

22. The time your daughter made you a handmade Father's Day card that you cherished for years to come.

23. The family BBQ where your daughter took charge of the grill and impressed everyone with her culinary skills.

24. The day your daughter landed her dream job, and you couldn't contain your pride and excitement.

25. The time your daughter surprised you with a spontaneous road trip and you ended up making memories that would last a lifetime.

These anecdotes are sure to add warmth, humour, and nostalgia to the father of the bride's speech, creating a memorable and heartfelt moment for everyone at the wedding.

Chapter 6 - "Father of the Bride: The Ultimate Jokester"

These jokes are sure to bring laughter and light-heartedness to the wedding celebration, making it a day to remember for the happy couple and their guests.

1. "Why did the father of the bride wear sunglasses to the wedding? Because his daughter's future is so bright, he had to shield his eyes!"
2. "What do you call a father who's just walked his daughter down the aisle? Relieved!"
3. "Why did the father of the bride bring a ladder to the wedding? He heard the bride and groom were tying the knot!"
4. "Why did the father of the bride give the groom a watch? Because it's about time he took his daughter off his hands!"
5. "Why did the father of the bride bring a map to the wedding? In case he needed directions to give his speech!"
6. "Why did the father of the bride wear sneakers to the wedding? He wanted to be prepared in case he had to run off with the bride!"
7. "What's the father of the bride's favourite dance move? The 'dad shuffle'!"
8. "Why did the father of the bride bring a thermometer to the wedding? To check if the groom had cold feet!"
9. "Why did the father of the bride bring a calculator to the wedding? To keep track of how much the wedding is costing him!"
10. "Why did the father of the bride bring a pillow to the wedding? In case he needed to take a nap during the speeches!"
11. "Why did the father of the bride bring a parachute to the

wedding? In case he needed to bail out during the father-daughter dance!"

12. "Why did the father of the bride bring a dictionary to the wedding? To make sure he didn't 'misspell' his speech!"

13. "Why did the father of the bride bring a toolbox to the wedding? To fix any 'marriage glitches' that might arise!"

14. "Why did the father of the bride bring a magnifying glass to the wedding? To 'focus' on the happy couple!"

15. "Why did the father of the bride bring a stopwatch to the wedding? To make sure the speeches didn't drag on too long!"

16. "Why did the father of the bride bring a life jacket to the wedding? In case he got 'swept away' by the emotion of the day!"

17. "Why did the father of the bride bring a flashlight to the wedding? To 'shine a light' on the happy couple's future!"

18. "Why did the father of the bride bring a rubber chicken to the wedding? To 'squawk' up some laughs during his speech!"

19. "Why did the father of the bride bring a fishing rod to the wedding? In case he needed to 'reel in' the groom!"

20. "Why did the father of the bride bring a map to the wedding? To show the groom where the 'point of no return' is!"

21. "Why did the father of the bride bring a bell to the wedding? To 'ring in' the start of the celebrations!"

22. "Why did the father of the bride bring a telescope to the wedding? To get a 'closer look' at his daughter's happiness!"

23. "Why did the father of the bride bring a deck of cards to the wedding? To 'deal' with any last-minute nerves!"

24. "Why did the father of the bride bring a dictionary to the wedding? To look up the definition of 'love'!"

25. "Why did the father of the bride bring a bouquet of flowers to the wedding? In case he needed to 'bloom' with pride for his daughter!"

Chapter 7 – A Father's Love: Poems from the Heart

These poems reflect the depth of a father's love for his daughter and the special bond they share. They can add a touch of sentiment and emotion to the father of the bride's speech, creating a memorable and heartfelt moment for everyone at the wedding.

"A Father's Love: Poems from the Heart"

Opening

As I stand here today, with joy and pride,
To celebrate my daughter, my heart's guide.
With words of love and memories to share,
I offer these poems, with tender care.

"Daddy's Little Girl"

My little girl, so grown and fair,
With eyes that sparkle, beyond compare.
From the moment you were born, my heart did swell,
And in your laughter, all my worries fell.
Today you stand before me, a radiant bride,
Ready to embark on life's greatest ride.
Though you'll always be my little pearl,
I'll cherish forever my daddy's little girl.

"To My Daughter on Her Wedding Day"

My dearest daughter, on this special day,
I give you my love in every way.
As you walk down the aisle, so pure and bright,
I'm filled with joy and sheer delight.
You've grown into a woman, strong and true,
And now you start a life anew.
Though you'll always be my baby, small,
Today, I give you to your love, to stand tall.

"Forever Yours"

With every step you take, my dear,
Know that my love is always near.
Through every laugh, through every tear,
I'll hold you close, year after year.
Your wedding day, a bittersweet sight,
As I watch you shine in love's pure light.
But though you start a journey new,
Know that I'll always be here for you.

"A Father's Blessing"

Today, my daughter, I give to you,
A father's blessing, pure and true.
May your life be filled with love and grace,
And joy shine bright upon your face.
May your marriage be a bond so strong,
Where you both belong, where you both belong.
And as you start this life anew,
Know that my love will see you through.

"In Her Eyes"

In her eyes, I see the stars,
A universe that's all her own.
In her smile, I find my joy,
A love that's never known to roam.
On this day, as she becomes a wife,
I'll hold her close with all my might.
For though she leaves, my love remains,
A bond unbroken, forever unchained.

"Always and Forever"

My darling daughter, hear my vow,
To love and cherish you, here and now.
Though you leave to start a life anew,
Know that my love will follow you.

In every moment, big or small,
I'll be there to catch you when you fall.
For though you're grown and far from me,
You'll always be my baby, you'll always be.

Chapter 8 – "A Father's Wisdom: Navigating Life's Journey with Love and Grace"

As the father of the bride, you hold a wealth of wisdom and life experiences that you've gathered along your journey. Your daughter's wedding day marks not only the beginning of a new chapter in her life but also an opportunity for you to share your insights and guidance as she embarks on this beautiful journey of marriage.

My dearest daughter,

As I stand before you today, watching you radiate with happiness and love, my heart swells with pride and joy. From the moment you entered this world, you have filled my life with immeasurable blessings, and I am grateful for every precious moment we have shared together. Today, as you embark on this new chapter of your life, I want to share with you some words of wisdom that I hope will guide you and inspire you as you journey through the beautiful adventure of marriage.

First and foremost, always remember the power of love. Love is the foundation upon which all great relationships are built, and it has the strength to overcome any obstacle that may come your way. Cherish the love you share with your partner, nurture it, and let it be the guiding force in your life. Love unconditionally, forgive freely, and never underestimate the transformative power of a kind word or a gentle touch.

Communication is key in any relationship, my dear. Always strive to communicate openly and honestly with your partner, sharing your thoughts, feelings, and dreams with one another. Listen with an open heart, and never be afraid to express your needs or concerns. Remember that true intimacy is built on a foundation of trust and understanding, so make communication a priority in your marriage, and never take the gift of honest dialogue for granted.

Trust your instincts, my darling. You possess an inner wisdom and intuition that will guide you through life's twists and turns. Listen to that still, small voice within you, and trust yourself to make the right decisions, even when the path ahead seems uncertain. Believe in your own strength and resilience and know that you are capable of overcoming any challenge that comes your way.

Never stop growing and learning, my precious daughter. Life is a journey of discovery, and there is always something new to learn, experience, and explore. Embrace each day as an opportunity for growth, and never be afraid to step outside of your comfort zone. Seek out new adventures, challenge yourself to try new things, and never lose your sense of curiosity and wonder.

Remember the importance of gratitude, my dear. Take time each day to count your blessings, and never lose sight of the many gifts that life has bestowed upon you. Cultivate an attitude of gratitude, and let it fill your heart with joy and contentment. Gratitude has the power to transform even the darkest of days into moments of light and beauty, so always be mindful of the blessings that surround you.

Be kind and compassionate, my darling. In a world that can sometimes be harsh and unforgiving, choose kindness and compassion as your guiding principles. Treat others with respect and empathy and strive to make a positive difference in the lives of those around you. Remember that a kind word or a simple act of kindness has the power to brighten someone's day and make the world a better place.

Take care of yourself, my precious daughter. Remember that self-care is not selfish, but rather a necessary component of living a happy and fulfilling life. Prioritize your physical, emotional, and spiritual well-being, and make time for the activities and practices that nourish your soul. Remember that you cannot pour from an empty cup, so take time to replenish your own energy and vitality.

Embrace the beauty of imperfection, my dear. None of us are perfect, and we all make mistakes from time to time. Embrace your flaws and imperfections as part of what makes you uniquely beautiful and extend the same grace and compassion to others. Remember that it is through our struggles and challenges that we grow and evolve, so never be afraid to embrace your humanity and vulnerability.

And finally, my precious daughter, always remember that you are loved beyond measure. No matter where life's journey may take you, know that my love for you is unwavering and unconditional. I am here for you, always and forever, cheering you on, supporting you, and believing in you every step of the way.

With all my love,

Your Father

As we come to the end of "From the Heart: Father of the Bride Speeches," I hope you have found inspiration and guidance in crafting a speech that truly reflects the depth of your love and affection for your daughter on her wedding day.

Writing and delivering a father-of-the-bride speech is a momentous occasion—one filled with emotion, reflection, and celebration. It's an opportunity to express your pride and joy as you witness your daughter embark on this new chapter of her life and to offer words of wisdom and guidance as she begins her journey as a married woman.

Throughout this book, we've explored the art of crafting a memorable and meaningful speech, from finding inspiration and structuring your thoughts to delivering your words with sincerity and authenticity. We've discussed the importance of speaking from the heart, expressing your emotions openly and honestly, and celebrating the unique bond you share with your daughter.

Above all, we've emphasized the importance of love—expressing your love for your daughter in words that are heartfelt, genuine, and sincere. Your daughter's wedding day is a celebration of love, and your speech is an opportunity to share in that celebration, to honour the love between your daughter and her partner, and to express your love for your daughter in a way that is both meaningful and memorable.

So, as you prepare to deliver your speech, remember to speak from the heart, to let your love for your daughter shine through in every word you say. And above all, remember that your daughter's wedding day is a day to celebrate love in all its forms—to rejoice in the bonds of family and friendship, and to cherish the moments of joy and laughter that fill the air.

Thank you for joining me on this journey and may your father-of-the-bride speech be a testament to the love and affection you hold for your daughter, now and always.

With warmest wishes,

Disclaimer:

The contents of this book, "From the Heart: Father of the Bride Speeches," are intended for informational purposes only and should not be considered a substitute for professional advice. The information provided in this book is based on the author's personal experiences and opinions, and readers are encouraged to consult with a qualified professional for specific guidance tailored to their individual circumstances.

While every effort has been made to ensure the accuracy and completeness of the information presented in this book, the author and publisher make no representations or warranties of any kind, express or implied, about the suitability, reliability, or accuracy of the contents. The author and publisher disclaim any liability for any loss or damage resulting from reliance on the information contained herein.

Readers are advised to use their own judgment and discretion when applying the suggestions and recommendations provided in this book. The author and publisher shall not be held responsible for any consequences arising from the use of the information presented in this book.

Furthermore, the names, characters, and events depicted in this book are purely fictional and any resemblance to actual persons, living or dead, or events is purely coincidental.

By reading this book, you agree to indemnify and hold harmless the author and publisher from any and all claims, damages, losses, liabilities, costs, and expenses arising from your use of the information contained herein.

Thank you for your understanding and cooperation.

Milton Keynes UK
Ingram Content Group UK Ltd.
UKHW022349231024
450133UK00001B/129